AT HOME

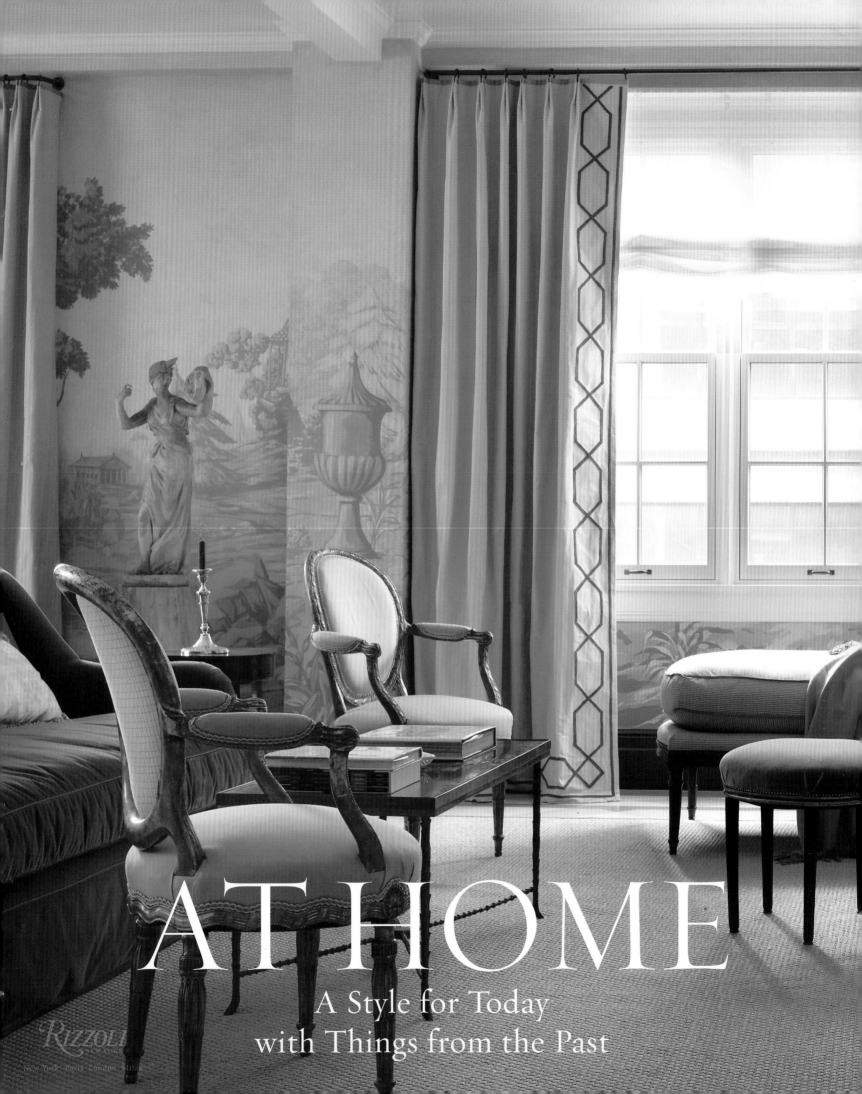

AT HOME

A Style for Today
with Things from the Past

RIZZOLI
New York · Paris · London · Milan

SUZANNE RHEINSTEIN

PHOTOGRAPHY BY PIETER ESTERSOHN

*For my husband, for my mother and my daughter, and
to the memory of my grandmothers—with deepest thanks
for your love, inspiration, and encouragement.*

For my dear friends who shared their houses for this book.

Contents

FOREWORD

Daily life at a design magazine frequently involves navigating people and places that proclaim their fabulousness with great fanfare. That is not the case, however, when working with Suzanne Rheinstein, who has inspired me for nearly two decades, ever since I was a junior editor and first visited Hollyhock, her stylesetting home-furnishings emporium in Los Angeles. Razzle-dazzle rooms have never been this decorator's calling card; on the contrary, she crafts sublime spaces rich with polish and patina and layered with nuance. Her world is one ruled by understated elegance, and Suzanne's clients—who often as not become her close friends—benefit from her gimlet eye, flawless taste, and uncommon attention to detail. The interiors she conjures for them convey an enchanting sense of personal history, revealing their beauty and provenance with a quiet confidence.

Just as Hollyhock is a beloved source for decorating essentials, the Georgian Revival house that Suzanne shares in Los Angeles with her debonair husband, Fred, is the ultimate design lab for living the good life. That is, if the good life is reflected by low-key luxe, uncompromising comfort, and furnishings with a breezy lack of pretense despite their fine pedigree. Here, mindfulness is key, from the very moment the Rheinsteins' front door opens onto a spacious hall whose stately millwork is punctuated by scarlet grosgrain trim. This is a deeply seductive setting, especially during their frequent parties: The air is fragrant with roses, deep-dish upholstery beckons, silver candelabra glimmer and gleam, jazz plays softly, and lanterns and votives flicker in the magical gardens surrounding the house. Truth be told, of the thousands of homes I've visited throughout my career, Fred and Suzanne's is perhaps the one I treasure most.

Though she's known for her refined, discriminating taste and graceful manner—Suzanne is *not* a casual woman—her mind-set is surprisingly down-to-earth. "I've never been daunted by having people over," she once told me. "Just make simple food and have lots of it, and put out a million candles. Candles hide a multitude of sins." Such smart and savvy advice is sprinkled throughout *At Home*. Its refreshingly personal prose complements Pieter Estersohn's extraordinary photographs of the Rheinsteins' Hancock Park house and Manhattan apartment, as well as a wide range of compelling projects Suzanne has completed across the country. Let this remarkable book be your perfect primer not simply to decorating beautifully, but—an even more difficult art, and one that Suzanne makes appear effortless—to living well.

—Margaret Russell
Editor in Chief, *Elle Decor*

INTRODUCTION

I cannot remember a time when I wasn't interested in my surroundings. As a small child I loved being in our garden, which my mother designed and my father tended to keep our house filled with flowers. 'Cecile Brunner' roses, camellias, bridal wreath, and wisteria were all part of it, with a deliciously minty patch of green beneath the water spigot. Osmanthus—sweet olive—was my climbing tree and the true scent of my childhood. I do believe many gardens are about memories. I know that mine is.

We moved into our late-Victorian house when I was five. The endless, dark-brown woodwork was varnished, with crocodile crazing on the surface, and the rooms were gloomy. Before long Mother arranged to have the woodwork pickled a light gray downstairs and painted upstairs, and the house began to feel young. I loved our especially sunny kitchen, which was not fitted with cabinets all around the way they are today. Instead, there was a freestanding stove by the old chimney, a cabinet with a sink, and a big, round breakfast table in the corner. The floor was checkered red and black, and long yellow curtains framed the tall windows, which in true fifties fashion had glass shelves with a collection of potted succulents. To this day I love kitchens decorated like rooms.

Our house had a wide staircase, which continued up to an attic used for storage. Mother had arranged neat stacks of *Vogue*, *House & Garden*, *Gourmet*, and *Flair* on these steps and I adored looking at those magazines. I also liked setting the table for dinner and looking at the old monogrammed porcelain and silver pieces that she had inherited from her great-grandmother, who had gone to live in the Yucatán from Spain when she was five. Her name was Eloisa and she was known for her style. Her daughter, another Eloisa, my mother's grandmother, who brought her own family to New Orleans from Mexico, was the one who gave her love of flowers to my mother, and taught her how to arrange them and set a beautiful table.

My brother, who grew up to be an architect, didn't come along until I was in my teens. We lived only a few more years in our house before the family scene began to loosen and disintegrate. Mother went to work and eventually became a partner in an antiques shop and began to decorate professionally. She was a model for me, as I decided to go back to work after our daughter was in school. People would ask me to do their houses the way I had designed our house. Eventually I opened Hollyhock, a small shop selling antiques and other interesting things for the house. From this beginning, Suzanne Rheinstein and Associates has grown.

The house my husband, Fred, and I share in Windsor Square has always reflected what is dearest to us—having a comfortable and attractive house that is welcoming to our friends and family no matter how spontaneous the visit. I strongly believe that how you live your life every day is so much more important than getting your house together for a special occasion. A party house shouldn't really look that different from your everyday house.

I remember reading the *L.A. Times Book Review* one lazy Sunday morning in the seventies and coming upon a quote from Joan Didion that has never left me. The interviewer made a comment about how she was known for using her good silver every day, and she replied, "Every day is all there is." I kept that page folded in my wallet until it disintegrated. Those words seemed so true to me in many ways, then, and now. On a material level, they remind me to appreciate and take pleasure in all the things I choose for daily life—the all-white, eco-friendly toothbrush I recently discovered and our simply shaped drinking glasses from a catalog as much as our antique creamware plates. All are a daily habit.

I have been fortunate that, along the way, I learned so much from so many people. Together, Fred and I have explored the architecture of so many cities. And because he brought me here, my fascination with color and light is stoked every year when the gorgeous, slanting winter sun of Southern California makes its appearance. Going with friends to faraway places, like the glaciers of Patagonia, leaves memories of dreamy color that recur in my designs. And always, for me, there are gardens. I have been taken to visit so many kinds of gardens—large and small, spare and abundant—through generous friends and through the Garden Conservancy, and I always take an idea away with me.

It was through gardens that my friendship with Courtnay Daniels first blossomed, and they have been a theme of our friendship. Soon after meeting, we volunteered to work in the herb garden at the Huntington Botanical Gardens with a group of older women who mentored us. We worked there every week until I was too pregnant to kneel down and weed and the Daniels moved to another city. The moving force in these weekly gatherings was Ruth Morley, from whom I first learned about shrub roses, brown iris, and Meyer lemons and who gave me so many slips of perennials for my fledgling garden. She had a style all her own, with an extravagant, never-wired, eighteenth-century French crystal chandelier in her family's living room and the sofas covered in real, striped awning fabric. When she gave a large party, she had wide, shallow white bowls that we used instead of plates; beautiful, long silver forks; and starched, generous napkins to put on our laps. I was in heaven.

All of these life experiences have influenced the way I work. As I usually design for families who really live in their houses, with children and pets, I hold comfort and livability high. So, too, do I hold the search for interesting or unusual pieces to make each room unique rather than ordering in rooms full of furniture from a showroom or catalog. My preference is for antiques and one-of-a-kind objects, gathered over time. The rooms I design are object driven, which could be a weather-beaten stool for the porch or a fine kettle stand for a chair-side table. With a personal collection of well-chosen furniture, a family can radically change colors over the years, be spare or chockablock, formal or less so, and still use the same good furniture. It is a matter of quality over quantity, or, as I am known to tell my young associates, I believe in "fewer things, but better things."

I have enjoyed sharing these special rooms with you—rooms that summarize what I love most in design. In the end, as my friend William Yeoward says, all design is an opinion, and this happens to be mine.

IN-TOWN GEORGIAN REVIVAL

Walking up to our house in the Windsor Square section of Hancock Park for the first time, in the twilight of a January Sunday, my husband, Fred, decided that this was where he wanted us to live. We made an offer that night and moved in two months later. We arrived with the furniture from our much-loved house in the Hills and a month-old babe in our arms. That was some thirty years ago, and ever since it has been a most wonderfully accommodating house for the way we live.

Begun in 1914, the house was designed by the Milwaukee Building Company, which later became Meyer and Holler, in the Georgian Revival style with rigorous classical details. Its beautifully proportioned rooms—not too large or grand—are one reason people feel so comfortable being here. The entry hall is welcoming. Light pours in from all sides, and it is large enough for the old Chickering piano from Fred's childhood home. For larger gatherings, we usually have our favorite jazz pianist, Geoff Aymar, playing to welcome guests.

On one side of the entry hall is the living room. I am usually a strong advocate for actually living in living rooms, but we do not. We do use the room when we have friends over, and that is often, as dear friends live next door, across the street, and around the blocks of Windsor Square. If we are having just a few people for dinner, we might light a fire and the candles in the room and serve drinks there. If we have invited a crowd for a buffet supper or a festive Southern-style breakfast, they usually spread out here and all over the first floor, including the back porch as well as up and down the stairs, stadium style. There are easy-to-move chairs in the living room, mostly French, to form small groups of diners.

A blue-gray color was used to stipple and glaze the walls of the living room and when the final protective coat went up, it turned a blue-green, which I decided to regard as a happy accident. Much of the furniture in this room was collected by my husband's parents for the house they built in New York City, where Fred grew up. They both had marvelous style and informed taste, and we love the things we have that were theirs. One of them, a yew-wood secretary, we have filled with books, with more stacked on the pullout writing surface. The handsome stripped-pine Georgian mantel also came from their house.

Los Angeles is a place that is cool in the evenings and mornings and becomes warmer in the middle of the day. Our house was built at a time when attention was paid to the climate, so we rarely have to use the air-conditioning. We prefer opening the windows to the breeze when it is warm, and sweaters and fires at night. Living this way makes the house more alive with movement.

The houses in Windsor Square were built in different architectural styles, which have retained their integrity as, fortunately, this neighborhood's preservation designation protects the character of the facades. Our house was begun in 1914 in the middle of a bean field. RIGHT: Looking from the entrance hall to the living room, with the seating in its striped summer slipcovers. The straw rug sometimes stays year-round, as I like the contrast with the rich wood and paint of the antiques. The eighteenth-century mirror's plate shows the ravages of time, an effect I love.

I painted the paneling in the way it might have been painted in Georgian times, in various shades of white for depth, with the baseboards and stair risers in a deep, bronzed brown. Portraits—seventeenth-century Dutch, nineteenth-century English, and eighteenth-century Italian—hang on the diaper-patterned linen walls and beyond. Red grosgrain ribbon outlines the linen in a lighthearted reference to the gilt fillets in authentic Georgian rooms. RIGHT: The red baize door, with nail-head panels, muffles noise from the butler's pantry. This is the time-honored European way of decorating such doors. My husband collected the Persian rugs early on, and they have always seemed just right in this room, as well as on the stairs.

Much of the art on the walls and the objects in the rooms were chosen when we were traveling and had the time to look and fall in love with what we saw. My husband doesn't care for contemporary art the way I do, but we can both agree on older things, especially portraits. In the downstairs living areas, we have a family of Venetian doges, nine of them, and a portrait of a European lady in an *orientaliste* mode, which we bought in Venice. We both adore that city and have spent a lot of time there, especially in the winter when there are fewer people and the atmosphere is moodier. In the entrance hall is a pair of starkly handsome seventeenth-century Dutch portraits and, in a very different style, a mid-nineteenth-century portrait of an English expatriate family in Italy.

I am always on the lookout for pieces made by women in the eighteenth century to amuse themselves. I have hung them throughout the rooms as a contrast to the paintings. Some are truly extraordinary, with work that is intricate and of a very high quality. Some are *coquillage* (designs with shells), *cartonnage* (intricately cut-out paper), *dessins habillés* (gouache figures "dressed" with bits of silk and gilt paper), or painted birds dressed with feathers. The gouache background paintings for these charming pieces could be ordered from shops in London and Paris and then decorated in a woman's chosen style at home.

I am also under the spell of reverse-glass paintings, especially the ones done in the eighteenth and early nineteenth centuries in Italy. I swooned when I saw over three hundred of them scattered throughout the stunningly chic Villa del Balbianello on Lake Como. *Capriccios* (architectural fantasies) with flower-bedecked lovers surrounded by sheep and oxen in front of classical ruins are painted with loose brushstrokes and gorgeous colors. These pieces are usually small and often whimsical. I also have reverse-glass paintings from China. These are more serious portraits, like the ones we have of European subjects, painted from engravings.

I love the graphic shapes of the French chairs and the Regency sofa and tables, and the stained or painted or gilded surfaces in the living room. We always light the candles when we are here in the evening, whether for predinner drinks for four, or a buffet supper for forty. The finials on the curtain poles were copied from painted Regency ones found at O. F. Wilson in London.

The Charles Garabedian collage painting moved right into this spot more than thirty years ago. In front of it is a painted Italian table that Gep Durenberger found for us, and a headless bust from the eighteenth century. The gilt chair is a pastiche of styles, not period, but loved nevertheless. The living room is a party room, not for lolling or long reading sessions. It gets soft morning light, shining here on a vase filled with spring sweet peas.

The living room, with its cool-weather upholstery of silks, velvet, and French printed cotton, has a view to the entrance hall and the dining room. The two nineteenth-century painted-wallpaper panels were taken from the dining room of my husband's childhood house. I enjoy bringing cuttings from the garden to arrange throughout the house and often prefer foliage to flowers in the downstairs rooms. I love the dark-blue berries of myrtus and the bright colors of coleus in the summer.

Next to the yew-wood secretary is a painted Italian chair with an embroidered cushion. Above it is a reverse-glass painted portrait of a lady in a bonnet. Here is a detail of the curtains, a linen-and-silk mix, trimmed in cotton fringe and tape, lined in the little check traditionally used on the backs of French upholstery. Two eighteenth-century Chinese gouaches hang below a reverse-glass Chinese mirror painting. Sitting on the Italian olive wood *comodino* is a *decalcomania* vase—ladies would cut and paste printed images to the inside of glass vessels in imitation of Chinese porcelain. RIGHT: Nine portraits of Venetian doges hang above a northern Italian chest.

From the living room, there is a wide passage into the library, added in the 1930s. This painted
and paneled room has the same classic proportions as the rest of the house and is where
we hang out at night, reading or playing dominoes and cards. It has the squishiest sofas
in the house and a great television. Eating a Sunday night supper off a tray in here is heaven,
especially with a blazing fire. The portrait of our daughter, Kate, is by Isabel Wadsworth.

Entertaining

On the other side of the entry hall is the dining room, with walls painted in stripes of glazing liquid, so that they are translucent. The Russian chandelier catches the light, too. I used a collection of watercolors of various English birds, from an ornithological treatise from about 1805, and framed them in hand-rolled glass with imperfections that unevenly refract the light and have the soft reflections of eighteenth-century glass. The silver is mostly old Sheffield plate, so the reflections are soft, not bright—my favorite pieces are those with the copper bleeding through. The Regency mahogany table is perfect for us, as it can seat up to sixteen people and also comes apart, so we can have four forty-eight-inch round tables in the room for celebratory dinners, with eight guests closely seated around each one. Bamboo chairs are brought down from the attic for these occasions.

Behind the dining room are the butler's pantry and the kitchen. We resolved to open up these spaces, once isolated and meant for servants, to the rest of the house, creating a new back-of-house way of living while respecting the original architecture. The kitchen connects to our former sunroom, which leads to a gallery connecting to the library. The kitchen now looks as if it is part of the house, since the small appliances that would normally crowd the counters are stored in a service porch right off of it. I don't usually like the look of hanging cabinets in a kitchen and find that the counters beneath them quickly fill with clutter. Instead, there is a shallow built-in pantry, floor to ceiling, that was original to the kitchen and which we retrofitted for better storage. A large table in the middle of the room serves equally well with lots of people around it, chopping, or, as is usually the case, just the two of us.

The watercolors of English birds were painted by the members of one family in England, around 1805. The gilding of the frames is softly rubbed so that black shows through in places. A three-tiered dumbwaiter holds forks and napkins so that guests can help themselves after they have filled their plates around the table. I buy huge, old monogrammed damask napkins, and use them for buffet parties.

The dining room is set up for a festive breakfast buffet of Southern dishes. It has lovely morning sunlight that enhances the glaze-painted walls and the old mirror, glass, and Sheffield plate silver. At night, candlelight has the same effect. Two nineteenth-century French terra-cotta garden statues are the newest addition but look as though they have always been there.

During a visit to Moscow in the 1980s, while touring beautiful historic houses and palaces, we came to appreciate the magic of the lighting in these dark, Baltic countries. We were happy to find this sparkling Russian chandelier on our return. The soft sheen of the silver plate on copper and the restrained shapes of these early candlesticks are appealing. RIGHT: The tape appliquéd to create a Greek key border is the same color as the wool-satin curtains, as I wanted it to be a quiet detail.

It took a while to figure out how to open up the kitchen to the rest of the house while still respecting the historic architecture by the Milwaukee Building Company. We kept the 1929 Magic Chef stove and took cues from the existing millwork, which, appropriately, was plainer than that in the public rooms of the house. We painted the millwork drab, a color traditionally used in the back of the house. The walls were painted a rich golden yellow and the table, turkey red. The original floor was striped with paint in various colors. RIGHT: A butler's pantry is a room to treasure. We retrofitted the cabinets with pullout shelves for plates and linens. A rolling ladder helps with reaching the higher storage. A bar, essentially bottles on an old tole tray, is set up at the far end; beneath it, behind the curtain, are refrigerators and wine cooling units, with spaces for cartons of drinks.

Back-of-House

The new back-of-house continues with the former sunroom (which is now rather shady after our remodel) that contains three bookcases filled with books on gardens. Our original dining room table and two wing chairs, chosen by my mother for our first house, reside in this room. These chairs have had numerous slipcovers and been used in various rooms over the years. Today, covered in a large-scale, crewel-embroidered cotton from my Lee Jofa collection, they are a great place to sit with books and catalogs, planning the garden, or with a computer. We also like to use this room for small winter dinners with a few friends. Everyone serves themselves from platters set out buffet-style on the kitchen table right next door.

When Fred and I are alone, I often arrange dinner on two trays and we decide which area of the house we want to dine in. For me, it seems easier to set an attractive tray than a table, and I enjoy using dishes, glasses, and napkins that I may only have a few of. Sometimes we take our trays outside to the porch or terrace. But if eating at a table, we almost always choose the one in the gallery, which is an extension of the library, the room where we spend most of our time when we are at home. We wouldn't miss breakfast at that table, as it looks out onto the garden. From here, it is easy to spot the first February rose on the roof of our Back House or the tiny native iris that bloom a few inches from the ground.

When reconfiguring the back of the house, we made this hallway serve as an entrance from the back porch into the house and kitchen. The ceiling angle on the right was changed to match the one on the left, a result of the back stairs. Shoes and hats for the garden are kept here, as well as lanterns for outside. The American portrait of a girl came to us from Fred's mother and the coffer, from my mother. I found the old patinated-metal pumpkin in Virginia.

Three gouaches decorated with feathers hang above a painted, decoupage Italian cupboard. RIGHT: The sunroom is shadier after our remodeling, but it does get light through the French doors. FOLLOWING PAGES: The stone-floored gallery was once part of the outdoor area. A chinoiserie screen, printed in sepia and then painted, hangs above a chest of drawers, flanked by painted chairs, all eighteenth-century Italian. The carved-wood allegories of the four seasons are French. Our favorite place to eat is in front of this window overlooking the back garden. The table was our daughter's desk. The design of my small and comfortable June Street chair was based on a chair I found at a tag sale on June Street in the late 1980s.

Bedrooms

The old Persian rugs continue up the hall stairs as does the linen wall covering, which provides a warm backdrop for a collection of black-and-white engravings. All of the bedrooms open off this hall. For more than twenty-five years the master bedroom was furnished with a classic English country-house bed and curtains, made for us by Colefax and Fowler in their fuchsia pattern. The spark for rethinking the decor came from the new fabric collection I was designing for Lee Jofa at the time. Brecy, originally a French floral ikat silk document that I reinterpreted on soft cotton, was used for the new window curtains. There was a bed, bought long ago for its shape and painted finish, and stored in our attic, which I had lengthened and then upholstered in the pale-melon shade of my Glazed Silk fabric. Recovering old friends, such as the trefoil ottoman and a favorite chaise longue helped to make the room familiar, yet fresh. The trompe l'oeil paneling was retained and touched up. The most dramatic change was painting the floor in elongated octagons of *faux marbre*.

The two spare bedrooms are furnished for the comfort and delight of our guests. One has an iron *lit à la polonaise*, patterned after the drawings that Bunny Mellon used for the beds she had made for Evangeline Bruce and Jackie Kennedy Onassis. I love the contrast of the draped bed with the painted floor, almost covered in cream-colored hides. The curtains are in English hand-blocked chintz with a strong turquoise background and finished with the tiniest ruched lavender silk edging. They were made some ten years ago, after Bunny Williams arranged for a group of us to tour the private quarters of Marie Antoinette at Versailles. There, I was struck by the spare yet sumptuously thick curtains. This room also has a large Italian fruitwood bookcase with bronze screened doors containing hundreds of amusing and oddball memoirs and books on decorating, manners, eating, and gardening.

The other guest room is like a garden, with the curtains and duvet of different greens in Glazed Silk. The antique chair and ottoman are covered in Garden Roses, which I designed to look like hand-blocked linen, used on the reverse. The chandelier was bought at the Paris flea market. Made of hundreds of metal leaves painted various shades of green, it originally hung in a winter garden and had never been wired. Even the Italian table and chest in this bedroom are painted with flowers.

The upstairs hall is home to many different black-and-white engravings—these English worthies, engravings of "worthy" or prominent people, were bought in the 1980s in London. The iron lantern was found in Connecticut, and the Italian chest and French bergères at Tom Stansbury Antiques in Newport Beach, California. Masses of California pepper berry fill the wicker basket.

This master bedroom is the sum of what I love the most in design: fewer things but better things, painted surfaces, a mixture of furniture styles, a personal art collection, and attention to comfort, colors, textures, details, and light. The decor of this room was inspired by my Brecy fabric, which I used for the curtains.

In the dressing room, a poudreuse from my mother-in-law and pull-up window shades of taffeta, with the light streaming through. Pale spring stock banked with moss looks as if it is growing in the little Chinese pots. Here is a detail of the curtains against the trompe l'oeil paneling. The bookcase was constructed to incorporate a pair of painted Directoire pilasters. An Elizabethan child's portrait hangs above it, and a collection of pinprick pictures has been placed down the side. RIGHT: The Italian horseshoe writing table and the Edwardian raisin-lacquered tea table contrast with the painted surfaces of the floor, walls, and bed. Above the headboard I hung some of my favorite embroideries and dressed pictures.

A guest room with a straw rug and shades is dressed in green curtains and flower-printed linen. A winter garden chandelier of painted tole leaves came from a Paris flea market. RIGHT: Hung above the Italian table are a framed basket of *cartonnage* flowers made from finely cut paper and two small Italian *capriccios*. A pair of carved Spanish colonial putti, paint gently peeling, has been placed above the bed. The peeling paint adds atmosphere and character to the pieces.

A japanned cabinet holds an Old Paris perfume bottle. Above it, *cartonnage* flowers in an oval frame and a souvenir of the Taj Mahal painted on ivory. Spring ranunculus bunched in Victorian cornucopia vases sit on the chest of drawers. Angelica Kauffman engravings have been hung on the wall inside of the bed's canopy. RIGHT: This guest room has a sumptuously dressed iron bed. Floors are painted with a geometric pattern and covered with hides. Turquoise block-printed chintz curtains decorate this room, along with various pieces of painted and lacquered furniture.

The Garden

When we set about making a garden in the back of the house, my husband's one request was that it be a "crisp" garden, not a tangle of overflowing plants. I have always loved green, architectural gardens and thought a cool, serene space to look out upon would be a wonderful complement to our busy lives. I drew and redrew the garden many times with my knowledgeable friend, Courtnay Daniels, incorporating favorite ideas from years of visiting gardens all over the world.

In the end, rather than do it myself, I chose to work with a professional, the garden designer and plantswoman Judy Horton. The main garden is simple with clipped hedges and shaped plants contrasting with the vines, roses, and climbing shrubs growing on the house. The plants are in many shades of green and gray, and some just happen to flower—the flowers are not their raison d'être. Around the pool, we placed tubs of citrus—kumquats, satsumas, and limes—and throughout the garden we have used edibles as ornamentals—three different kinds of figs, persimmons, loquats, apples, and Persian mulberries. Around the corner from the gravel garden, behind a baffle of quince and clipped myrtle, lies the secret garden, where I allow myself to depart from the serenity of the rest of the garden and plant things willy-nilly. Here are chartreuse tubs of black cherry tomatoes, dark-purple sweet peas, black hollyhocks from Monticello, dahlias, lablab, *fraise des bois*, and loads of herbs.

When we made the garden and the porch, we also turned a garage and chauffeur's quarters into the Back House, a place for gatherings and long Sunday lunches with friends. Big French doors open all the way so you feel part of the outdoors, looking out across the pool and its garden. In the warmer months, we put out tubs of black colocasia and chartreuse ipomoea and similarly colored coleus around the garden. We spend a lot of time on our covered back porch on hot days. It is a great place to eat and look out over the garden and the little pond.

Looking across the pool into the Back House, its French doors open to the breezes, with giant Burmese honeysuckle growing up the brick facade. The pots around the pool are filled with citrus for their bright, hot colors. RIGHT: A view into the secret garden, which is the place to plant all kinds of crazy, colorful things in contrast to the main garden, which is cool, green, and clipped.

We painted the varnished beadboard of the Back House, glued sea grass to its cement floor, and added French doors and a fireplace to create a big room for lazily hanging out with friends. Then we filled it with favorite old pieces that no longer had places in the house and covered them in my fabrics for Lee Jofa. The slipcovers in the foreground are in Indian Zag, based on a fine old textile I bought in Rajasthan.

Looking out to the pool garden and *Acrobat*, by the English sculptor Jamie Vann, at the far end. RIGHT: The table is set for Sunday lunch, with a rough-woven linen sheet from Provence used as a tablecloth. The plates, shaped like cardinals' hats, are from Belgium. The Belgian linen kitchen towels, monogrammed for someone's trousseau, are used as napkins. Their textured pattern makes a nice contrast to the simple glazed plates. I can always find small bits of berries, herbs, and flowers from the garden to fill the little lead vases.

BAYSIDE COLONIAL

The Belling house is situated on Newport Bay, across from a sandy beach, in an old enclave that was once filled with small summer cottages. From the windows of the house, and from the crow's nest at the very top, you can always see boats—yachts and sleek sailing vessels, the little sabots that the children race every afternoon, and Duffys, the slow electric boats with charming canopies that neighbors use for late afternoon rides around the Bay.

The house is Colonial Revival, with gray-stained cedar shingles and an American crispness, which suits the seaside location. The front door is a Dutch one, and the top of it is often left open to allow sunlight and breezes to enter the front hall, which is all white-painted paneling and dark wood floors.

I had known Phil and Shelley Belling for some time, through mutual friends, and admired their taste, but creating this house was our first collaboration. We worked with the admirable Los Angeles architects Tichenor and Thorpe, who were especially clever in getting light to reach the center of the house, which is sited on a small narrow lot, and who fulfilled the owners' brief for simple yet meticulous detailing.

To one side of the hall is the living room, which receives light from three sides. In the front, toward the bay, are triple-hung windows, just like those at Monticello. They can be raised up to form doorways to walk onto the terrace. On the opposite side of the room, French doors open to the patio, so it is perfect for indoor-outdoor Southern California living.

On the other side of the patio is the family room—the kitchen is on the third side—which also has French doors and a paneled fireplace. A wraparound banquette and the television make it the place for the young people of the house to bring their friends. At the family parties that the Bellings like to have, food can be arranged in the kitchen and guests flow all over the patio, the family room, and the living room, as well as through the entry hall and out into the front garden.

The Colonial Revival shingled house is across from a quiet sandy beach in Newport Bay. The house and its interiors are classically proportioned, contributing to its air of seaside serenity. RIGHT: The flood of light into the entry hall highlights the uncomplicated paneling and simple curve of the stair, the kind of restrained, meticulous detailing the Bellings wanted. Antique lighting was used throughout to give depth to the new construction.

A beautiful neoclassical mantel that Shelley discovered was the starting point for the living room. To contrast with the formal mantel, and because we loved the look, we used braided-rush matting on the floor and pretty, soft curtains in a taupe-and-white stripe that we hung on narrow poles. Comfortable upholstered and slipcovered pieces mix with antique chairs that can be pulled up to create different conversation groups. The walls and woodwork and overall feel of the room—and of the house—are all very fresh, and create a lovely foil to the mellow finishes of the antique furniture. Shelley likes a clean, spare room with not too many pieces of furniture or objects. We spent a good deal of time searching for decorations that had interesting properties but were not over-the-top. The mirror above the fireplace is a favorite find, a classic oval with a carved urn and restrained garlands in not-too-crusty eighteenth-century gilt. The sconces on either side were bought at auction and some of the crystals were removed to bring their flash down a bit.

The pictures on the walls were chosen with equal care. They include Chinese reverse-glass paintings with mirrored backgrounds, sophisticated eighteenth-century embroideries, and an absolutely marvelous *coquillage* picture of a hummingbird hovering near an urn overflowing with all kinds of flowers, which came from Tony Duquette's remarkable estate.

The pale-taupe walls, simple striped curtains, and braided-rush matting provide an understated background for a spare arrangement of antique tables and pull-up chairs, some painted and others with a dark-wood patina. The upholstery is especially comfortable. The pale greens, lavenders, and other colors of the fabrics were inspired by the hand-screened linen on the chair in the foreground.

A green lady's slipper orchid is nestled into a nineteenth-century French cachepot. RIGHT: The painted chair has a cushion of glazed linen with frayed tufts. Above it hang Chinese reverse-glass paintings in tarnished silver-leaf bamboo frames, whose mirrored backgrounds add light and sparkle to the room. The French doors on either side overlook the patio that brings sunlight to this space, as well as into the family room and the kitchen. The fireplace on the patio is lit by the family on cool Southern California evenings.

The objects in the living room have been carefully collected over the years and stand out in this room that gets sunlight from three sides. A bolster trimmed with silk tassles rests on a chair. The Italian pictures above the linen fauteuil are a combination of fine embroidery and painting on silk. A lacquered China trade tea table holds amethyst-glass carafes of hydrangeas. RIGHT: The extraordinary *coquillage* picture, made of many different kinds of shells, once belonged to Tony Duquette. A Hepplewhite tea table is used in front of the sofa rather than a coffee table. The lavender-gray pillow is trimmed with a folded, pleated ribbon. The gilded shell plate is Old Paris.

In this house, full of the blue skies and slanting light of a Southern Californian December, the traditional red-and-green Victorian Christmas doesn't seem right—it asks for a different kind of festive decoration. Sugared fruits are a perfect complement to the collection of old mercury-glass vessels that Shelley has assembled over the years. More of the silvery, sugared leaves are tucked into the evergreens that swag the mirror and mantel.

In the powder room, we hung a hand-blocked chinoiserie paper with whimsical follies and meandering vines made by the artisans at Adelphi. A neoclassical chest was adapted for the pewter sink. A mirror and sconces that Shelley had owned for a long time worked here, without looking too matched up. RIGHT: A wraparound banquette in the family room is perfect for watching television. A sailor's valentine of shells, paintings, and watercolors on the walls reflect the Bellings' love of sailing and the sea.

Feeding Family and Friends

In contrast to most of the rooms on the ground floor, the cozy dining room, which also serves as the library, is paneled and snug as a ship. It is clad in waxed pine the color of pecans, and hung with "woolies," portraits of ships embroidered in wool yarn by sailors in the nineteenth century. They, and the shelves filled with books, give the room a mellow atmosphere. The French table and Italian chairs are fruitwood, and two linen upholstered wing chairs are at the ready for serious reading. Family meals are enjoyed at the kitchen table, in a windowed bay. When meals are served in the dining room—or a buffet is arranged there—the flicker of candles is reflected in the wood. For all of the rooms of this house, we searched for distinctive old lighting fixtures to give depth to the new construction. The French country chandelier is rustic in a charming way, with its armature and leaves and flowers of painted metal, and its rough crystals strung upon it for sparkle. The antique Delft tiles on the fireplace slips also add to the sense of history.

The kitchen is airy and full of light, painted an off-white, with the same dark-stained wood floors as in the rest of the house. The architectural detailing is rigorous and simple, without an elaborate cornice molding, but with a more appropriate planked ceiling painted a pale blue. Traditional marble counters and backsplashes were chosen, with a rich stained mahogany top used on the island. Over the years, Shelley has collected vintage white pottery vessels to use as decoration and storage for the produce, utensils, sponges, and the like. They help make the everyday beautiful.

Between the kitchen and the dining room is a gem of a small pantry with shallow floor-to-ceiling cabinets for storing china, and opposite, a traditional butler's pantry with a stained-wood counter and a beautiful oval window. This is where the vases and containers are kept and the flowers or foliage are arranged for the house. When there is a party, it can also function as a serving bar.

The dining room also serves as the library. A rustic old French chandelier and antique Delft tiles on the fireplace slips add to the mellow feeling, as does the waxed pine paneling. The brass candlesticks, collected over a number of years, bring warmth and sparkle. The upholstered wing chair, one of a pair, is for serious reading.

Just a glimpse of the chandelier and the
Delft tiles are visible in this view of the
"woolie" over the fireplace. These pictures
of ships were made from yarn by sailors in
the nineteenth century. Local persimmons
fill a tureen, part of a set of nineteenth-
century English china with Imari designs
that also includes these plates. RIGHT: The
mantel holds old tole containers filled
with eucalyptus leaves and berries
that grow all over Southern California.

The light-filled kitchen is detailed simply. A collection of old white pottery containers, in use every day, adds a layer of interest, as does the purely decorative group of transfer-printed, ship-decorated luster jugs displayed on the windowsill. The lighting fixture over the island is an early nineteenth-century French oil lamp; the one in the hall was a hanging basket from a French winter garden that we electrified.

An informal lunch of soup and skinny baguette sandwiches is served on creamware, both old and new. The pitcher holds bunches of herbs. RIGHT: Comfortable old Windsor chairs surround an oak gateleg table in the light-filled bay in the kitchen. FOLLOWING PAGES: A shallow space is used for china storage. Opposite it is a traditional butler's pantry, with a mahogany counter and a deep sink for arranging flowers for the house. A beautiful, swiveling window lets in light while preserving privacy.

Lunch is served on the patio. Mismatched metal furniture, collected at various French flea markets, is painted a bronzed brown to unify it. A flowering *fraise des bois* plant, plucked from the garden, is used to decorate the table. RIGHT: The charming electric Duffy, ready for a quiet ride and informal meal on the bay.

Upstairs

The upper hall is filled with as much light as the lower one, thanks to the large window above the entry door, which looks out to the bay. Light continues down the hallway to the rear, which has been lined with shelves that hold hundreds of children's books, creating a wonderful elongated children's library, complete with a window seat with feather cushions for curling up and additional soft light from the window facing the patio.

The bedrooms of the Bellings' daughters are off this library hall, fitted out with interesting beds and just a few pieces of furniture, simple and classic, that can be used for the rest of their lives. The art in the bedrooms reflects their individual interests. I have always felt that children's bedrooms should not be decorated in a cartoonish way. Rather, they can be child friendly and still contain furniture and art that will stay with them as they grow. Our own daughter began collecting engravings and drawings at flea markets when she was nine, and she now has those youthful treasures on the walls of her own family's apartment.

The master bedroom, in the front of the house and furnished with just a few, well-chosen pieces, is a serene retreat from the Bellings' busy lives. The colors are the cool blues and grays of the coastal fog. The floor is bare and the curtains are embroidered in a restrained way. The room perfectly illustrates the idea of having fewer but better things. It was a delight to help Shelley find the special pieces for this room. There are painted wood fragments over the bed and some especially fine, early flower embroideries, one in silk chenille. A pair of dressed pictures was found in New York, the painted mirror came from a French flea market, and the Italian chest of drawers and painted table were found in local shops.

The large upstairs windows light up the landing and the rooms on either side—a study and the master bedroom. The unusual botanical images above the simple painted paneling are actual seaweed that had been found and pressed in the nineteenth century and framed with matting of gilded sand in the traditional English manner.

A long hall has been outfitted with bookcases and a cozy window seat for a children's library and reading nook. RIGHT: A daughter's room has just a few pieces of furniture that can be with her forever. A hand-screened linen print from Raoul in Santa Barbara makes a lively and fun contrast to the narrow-striped cotton on the walls and pull-up shades. The 1950s fashion illustrations are by Emlen Etting.

The master bedroom serves as a quiet retreat. The antique Italian chest of drawers is both practical and handsome. Above it is an old French mirror painted white, and two fine English eighteenth-century dressed pictures. A group of pale embroidered silk flower pictures are hung near a silvered, decoupage lamp from the forties. The gardenias came from the patio garden. RIGHT: Beneath the painted bedside table is a basket of periodicals and books for nighttime reading—the settee is reserved for the dogs of the household.

MOUNTAIN RETREAT

One thing you notice immediately about this Sun Valley house is the way it nestles comfortably into the surrounding landscape. The property borders on the vigorous Big Wood River in Sun Valley, Idaho, and the view across the land is straight to the spectacular evergreen-covered Bald Mountain.

Phil and Shelley Belling thought a great deal about the kind of holiday house they wanted for their family, long before they started plans to build. They wanted it to be smaller rather than larger, and to feature traditional details. It was important to them that the house be warm and inviting both in summer and winter. Essentially, though, they wanted it to be an easygoing house for a modern family actively involved in the outdoor life that is the glory of the area. It was interesting and satisfying—and a great deal of fun—collaborating with the Bellings and the architect, Janet Jarvis, to design this house.

We used a lot of beautiful natural materials, such as repurposed oak for the floor, which was given an oil finish that makes a floor age better and doesn't require a lot of upkeep. Everyone can come in with hiking boots or fishing and skiing gear without worries. There is handsome, rustic stonework on the fireplaces, both inside and out, and we used reclaimed wood for some of the walls. Where there is paint, colors were carefully chosen not to be assertive, and to evoke the colors outside. Even the flowers placed about the house are from the local farmers market or are wildflowers, grasses, and leaves that grow nearby.

The house has a strong sense of place. This is abetted by its immediate landscaping, which has been coaxed back into a style in keeping with the natural surroundings. A manicured lawn and flowerbeds would be an affront to the majestic mountain and river.

All the time we were planning and building, we were also gathering handmade pieces—some old and some new—for the house and the original cabin on the property, which is now used as the bunkhouse. Leatherwork hassocks, a bark-decorated Swedish table, a Mexican Colonial worktable with large rounded nails, and Austrian antler-leg stools are some of the items that give the rooms a unique feel. The idea was to create a place that is rustic, but not in the traditional Adirondack or hackneyed Western style, a house of the mountains but with a contemporary sensibility.

A two-story living room serves as the core of the house, with a tall stone fireplace and a balcony looking down from the second story. From the beginning, we knew we wanted to create a large, welcoming room that could accommodate children and friends and children's friends, but that would still feel good when there were only two or three people there. The rug is wool, woven in concentric squares of soft wheat and gold, with an inky blue and a little bit of red. The squares and colors were painted in our design studio and then sent off to Tibet to be woven. The sofa is long enough for lots of people to sit and watch the Super Bowl or other sporting events, and is covered in the softest corduroy. The television is housed in a pared-down cabinet I designed made of rusty-looking steel.

The house and the original cabin are nestled into the landscape of the Big Wood River. RIGHT: The painted banister detailing was original to the outlying cabin, which we turned into a bunkhouse. The furnishings were made in many places and periods, but they all combine to create a harmonious sense of place. Here, an American stoneware jar sits on a Louis XV walnut country table. The flowers used in the house are simple wild- or country flowers, such as this Queen Anne's lace.

Everyone is drawn to the central, two-story living room, furnished with comfortable places to sit and talk, play games, or watch sports on television. In the winter, the room has enveloping warmth, and during the summer, as here, it invites the outside in. Striped linen slipcovers are placed over the winter upholstery. Rustic pieces, including a Spanish table used for games, an English low table in front of the sofa, and a hollowed-out tree trunk used as a child's chair near the fireplace, help establish the room's individuality. It is easy to feel part of this room even when in the kitchen, which is just visible to the left, below the balcony.

The large stone fireplace is perfect for roaring fires. The logs are stored in the bottom half of a spare steel cabinet that also houses the television. In back of the very long sofa is an equally long table made from a single slab of tree trunk, with slotted legs for easy disassembly. On holidays, it serves as an auxiliary table, perfect for eighteen children eating around it. Or it can be pushed against the wall and used as a buffet beneath the eighteenth-century screen painted with an Austrian alpine hunt scene. The food is presented on a collection of rustic serving pieces, and the tables are decorated with materials gathered from the outdoors, evergreens and pinecones, which are attractive, easy, and feel right for this house.

It even has a hidden drawer for the remotes. The bottom holds firewood, which becomes a graphic decoration. The upholstered chairs swivel for easy conversation, and across from them are two Edwardian club chairs that were redone in sueded pigskin. A games table, with its wicker chairs and leather cushions, is always waiting.

The curtains are closed only on the wintriest of nights. We embroidered the ridged linen-and-cotton fabric with a chenille design down the middle of each panel, not on the leading edges, because of the configuration of the doors. The many different textures in this room quietly work to give it interest.

To one side of the living room, and completely open to it, is the games room. Its low ceiling makes it cozy, as do the curtains and the walls, which are lined in shooting cloth of a dusty olive green, a color taken straight from the outside. There are high, easy-to-move chairs to watch the action at the handsome pool table. The ceiling was too low for hanging lamps to illuminate the pool table, so we used small bronze outdoor lights above it, to avoid having to poke holes in the lovely reclaimed wood ceiling, an idea we repeated in several other rooms. A group of antlers, collected by the Bellings, was hung on the wall for a graphic decoration and to evoke an alpine atmosphere.

We wanted an individual look for this room as well, so we used a provincial Directoire painted buffet fitted with a patinated-metal sink as a bar, which seems more domestic and low-key than a built-in bar. The extra glasses and other supplies are kept in the cupboards beneath, and a handsome tray holding cocktail accoutrements is set out on top.

The entry area is contiguous to the living room and the games room and is the first glimpse you get of the house. It, too, is furnished with a restrained, sophisticated mix of rustic pieces and various textures—a bleached Continental table, pale terra-cotta balusters from an old enclosure, an eighteenth-century Spanish mirror with whitewashed carved oak leaves and acorns, and a *faux bois* cement jardinière from the 1920s, all set against the strong horizontal design of the old wood walls. To the left of the entry are the mudroom and the family room and to the right is the living room.

The family room is lined with old barn siding and the upholstery stays in the same range of colors. It has a serene air, with French doors leading to a stone terrace overlooking the river. The room is primarily used for watching movies or reading, the shelves filled with interesting books on the outdoor life of Idaho as well as classic novels. During holidays, the banquette has been filled with as many as eleven children happily watching movies.

In the games room, a painted country buffet serves as a bar, set against the cozy walls covered in shooting cloth of sueded cotton. An antique terra-cotta wine cooler holds casually arranged native grasses and wildflowers. There are a few decorative accessories in the house, and most relate to the rustic alpine setting, such as the horn box and the tusk-handled biscuit barrel.

The star attraction in the games room is the handsome pool table, which I designed inspired by an old engraving. (I prefer not to use the ones with large, bulbous legs.) The raised chairs with footrests were copied from an Edwardian tennis referee chair and provide a good view of the shots. A banquette supplies more seating and is covered in old-fashioned boiled wool, as are the cushions, though they are embroidered in a simple geometric design to carry through a bit of the living room's blue and red. Hand-thrown ceramic lamps by Christopher Spitzmiller in a contemporary ridged pattern flank the banquette. The cozy room, lined in shooting cloth, opens onto the two-story living room.

The entry, with stairs to the sleeping rooms to the left and the living room to the right. A view through a pair of bleached-horn candlesticks into the games room. The powder room, with vinylized linen covering the walls and a patinated-metal sink set in a horn-clad chest of drawers. RIGHT: A living room chair in its winter upholstery, with a Swedish tree-trunk table just visible behind it. The curtains with chenille embroidery, behind a Spanish Colonial work-table. The lamp is made from an Indonesian cloth-printing roller. Favorite landscapes hang on the wall of horizontal planks. Four antique Austrian antler-legged stools sit in front of the fireplace, and beyond the French doors is the Big Wood River. The symbol of the house is an evergreen tree, which appears on cards and linens.

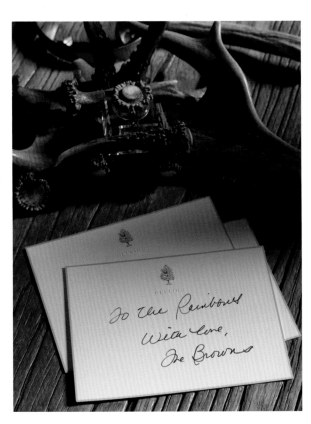

In the family room, the long banquette is covered in cotton and leather with lots of pillows. Only the two bolsters on the ends are fixed. The chairs are in hand-quilted linen slipcovers and the artisanal hassocks are suede. The colors of the fabrics come from the old barn siding lining the walls. RIGHT: An old French driftwood table has two photographs on the wall above it by Wilson "Snowflake" Bentley, the first photographer to take pictures of snowflakes in 1885. They were framed by the nonpareil framer Roger Lussier of Boston.

Easy Living

The kitchen opens onto the living room, yet is a little apart from it. We were all thoughtful about how it should look, since we wanted it to have a feeling similar to the rest of the house. At one end of the kitchen is the dining area, where everyone sits around an old Irish wake table. Some of the chairs are antique Windsors and some are Hollyhock Dining Chairs. They are upholstered in brown wool plaid, and wear these linen slipcovers when it is warmer. The chandelier is a modern design incorporating old mercury-glass-lined factory lights. It creates a clean-lined silhouette against the windows, which look out over the river. The same linen-and-cotton textured fabric used in the living room appears here at the windows as pull-up shades bound in blue. It is marvelous to have breakfast here with the windows open, with the sights and sounds of the Big Wood River rushing by, and the scents of the alpine trees wafting in.

The kitchen proper has the same repurposed wood floors and horizontal planks on the walls as the living room, and the same stone on the chimney breast. The cabinets are made of a different wood, with painted stiles and trim, to break up the wood and add visual interest. We cut down the size of the island that was originally proposed, as I have found that large ones are not practical or attractive in a family kitchen. By reducing the island we were able to incorporate a marvelous ancient Swedish table with a thick, old stone top. This table has so much more character, and is a great place to set out food for a party. On special occasions, the Bellings light the old hanging candleholder above the table.

The food laid out on the Swedish table personifies Sun Valley for me. The delicious smoked trout and crisp bread that is produced here and the Parmesan cheese chunks made famous by the local restaurant, Cristina's, are served with colorful yellow and orange carrots from the farmers market.

Upholstered dining chairs slipcovered for the summer mix with Windsor chairs around the antique Irish table in the kitchen's dining area. Here, in contrast to the kitchen proper, the walls are plastered. FOLLOWING PAGES: The old Swedish table is set with typical fare from the Sun Valley area. When the hanging candleholder is lit, the room becomes magical. Natural linen napkins are embroidered with the symbol of the house. On simple platters is the ideal food to enjoy with a glass of wine. The dining room chair wears its plaid winter upholstery. Right: A view over the island into the cozy kitchen fire. On the opposite side of it is an outdoor fireplace on the porch, which can be seen through the Dutch door.

Sleeping

All of the bedrooms are upstairs, off a hall with a balcony view of the living room. The hall is large enough to contain a great long table for a computer and a few club chairs for sitting, and makes the second story seem airy, though the bedrooms are not large.

The master bedroom is the only one with wood walls, which we painted celadon to blend in with the river and mountain view outside the mullioned doors. The bed is simply and comfortably made up with a soufflé-like blanket folded over the end woven by Sam Kasten. An adjoining bath is spacious and equally quiet, with softly colored paint and stone.

The guest room is subdued. Its rustic painted beds were made by Gep Durenberger, based on copies of antique ones he owned. Ticking-covered duvets dress the beds in the warmer months and linens in natural tones cover the windows and the furniture. The two daughters share a room with four bunk beds painted an alpine blue. A country table, a printed cotton chair, and a painted Austrian chest are among the few pieces of furniture in the room, so there is more space for kids. Overflow friends can sleep in the playroom, which has a pair of built-in beds and a closet full of sleeping bags. Families are usually put up in the bunkhouse.

The master bedroom, at the corner of the house, is filled with light. Its decoration is understated, with northern Italian painted bedside chests providing a bit of color. It defers to the view outside its second-story porch, which features a rustic-work railing and pediment.

An early nineteenth-century decoupage floral picture rests on a painted Italian chest of drawers. A corner of an herbarium page, framed in a corrugated-cardboard design. RIGHT: The light shines in on the master bath, which is flanked by tall mullioned cupboards. The towel is embroidered with the evergreen tree that is a symbol of the house. An antique armoire, a family heirloom, was lined with fabric and is used to store bed linens and towels in the adjacent hall.

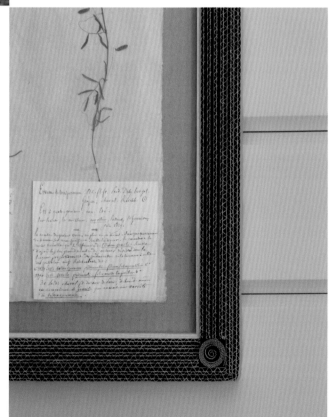

The playroom over the garage is reached by a wooden staircase from the mudroom. It is a great room for foosball, board games, or watching movies. Shearling beanbag chairs can be easily moved, and there are two built-in beds and plenty of places where kids in sleeping bags can bunk down during ski weeks.

Here are views of the guest room, which is furnished simply with handsome pieces, such as the old French invalid's chair, covered in hand-screened linen. A slatted cupboard built for clothes was painted smoky beige. It is like a piece of furniture rather than a built-in closet. The adjoining bathroom's stone and wood reiterates the same tones. RIGHT: The girls' room, with four bunk beds for sharing with friends, is fitted out with simple country furniture.

The mudroom is central to the activities of the house. Clad in wood and floored in stone, it is the place to store skiing, hiking, and fishing equipment. Divided drawers hold flies, but everything else is open. In the adjacent laundry room, the cabinet woodwork is painted a dusty sage green and topped with a teak counter, tolerant of moisture. Wooden bars for hanging soggy jackets to dry line one side of the room. RIGHT: Here is a special area for waders, jackets, and whatever else needs hanging.

By the River

As wonderful as the house is, it must bow to its outdoor setting. To be on a terrace or porch and view the swift-moving river against Bald Mountain, looking through the meadow that stretches to the water's edge, is powerful yet oddly calming. The river is used sometimes for tubing or canoeing and often for fishing, but now and then it serves simply as a backdrop for relaxing with family or friends. A wooden porch off the living room has a stone fireplace for cool days and evenings and is furnished with a group of old hickory chairs and other camp furniture. This is the perfect place for sandwiches or a predinner game of dominoes. Down the porch stairs and across a mowed patch of ground is the bocce court, where the Bellings bring out canoe chairs to sit on the grass to watch the players and perhaps have a picnic. In high summer, when the days are long, a beautiful bluestone table is piled high with tomatoes and vegetables from the local farmers market and something from the grill of the nearby barbecue. Lorna Lee and John Muller, who make modern interpretations of bark-clad branch furniture, crafted the chairs that surround the table. When it is time for complete indulgence, a hammock in the meadow grass next to the river is available for daydreaming.

The long bluestone table on the terrace overlooks the meadow grasses that edge the Big Wood River, with Bald Mountain rising steeply on the other side. The chairs are contemporary versions of American rustic furniture. Bounty from the barbecue grill and the farmers market is set out for a summer evening meal with friends.

The hammock in the meadow grasses by the river is the place to read—or pretend to read. The porch is filled with old rustic American camp furniture. Faux bois cement seating can be found in the grasses leading to the river. RIGHT: Old-fashioned canoe chairs surround a plaid blanket laid for a picnic. An outdoor lunch and a game of bocce are delightful ways to pass the afternoon, with the sound of the river in the background.

HORSE
COUNTRY
CLASSIC

Whilton Farm sits on almost three hundred acres in the foothills of the Blue Ridge Mountains in Virginia. The house is approached through gates and along a drive planted on either side with the same kind of tulip trees that Thomas Jefferson—that passionate gardener—grew a little farther south at Monticello. Between the trees you can glimpse the gardens and the fields that lead to the mountain, covered in beautiful yellow leaves in the fall, at the far edge of the farm.

After you park your car in the graveled courtyard, you look up to see a most welcoming old red-brick Georgian Revival house. Originally a simple farm cottage, it was redesigned in the 1930s by one of the architects who worked on the restoration of Williamsburg. He expanded the cottage and added eighteenth-century-style details, but it still retains the rambling layout of a farmhouse, which adds to its relaxed charm.

The owners of the farm, Courtnay and Terry Daniels, have been our friends for many years. While on a civic tour of Los Angeles, Courtnay and I met while standing in line to visit a women's prison. We laughingly bantered botanical Latin back and forth—in those days, *Verbena bonariensis* and its ilk did not trip off everyone's tongue the way they do now—and soon made a date to talk about gardens and books, and to pass on clippings from beloved plants. We discovered we shared an interest not only in those topics, but also in food, houses, and art. That was the beginning of a long friendship and, as our husbands also like each other, we have traveled many places as couples, as families, and as friends. Together, we have been inspired and learned so much—all while enjoying ourselves immensely. Our houses, and the way we live in them, have been much influenced by all of this.

When we first began to collaborate on decorating the farm, more than twenty years ago, we aimed for the mixture of comfort and beautiful objects that characterizes it today. Much of the upholstered furniture, although reupholstered, are the same classic designs that I first had made in my Los Angeles workrooms. The collections of antiques and art have grown, have moved from room to room, and some items have been passed on to children, but none have ever been discarded. They remain interesting and timeless.

The present look of the house was prompted by the wedding of a daughter. To me, there is nothing more wonderful than a wedding at the bride's family home. Whether many guests or few are invited, a wedding at home is an expression of a family's everyday hospitality writ large. By this time we had decorated Sunsong, their house in Florida, and Courtnay was so pleased with the quiet way it looked that she wanted to try a more low-key color scheme at the farm as well. It was engaging and exciting for me to be able to recolor the rooms and to rethink the arrangement of the marvelous furniture and art. We used all the family's existing furniture—an antique canapé migrated downstairs, sconces went upstairs, and favorite paintings now reside in the kitchen. Many familiar "friends" were installed in new places to be rediscovered and fallen in love with all over again.

The entry to the house is off a graveled motor court. Large and welcoming, the entry has places to drop your gear or to sit during long good-byes. Its checkered floors of green stone are friendly to the dogs that wander through and to riding boots and gardening shoes. Covering the walls, and continuing up the curving stairway, is wallpaper copied from one at Uppark, one of my favorite English country houses. From here, you step down into the living room that looks out to the spectacular Virginia countryside.

The living room was originally an old porch. We had its handmade brick floors waxed to a soft sheen and then covered them with a thick layer of rush matting made by the English apple growers during their off-season. The room contains many beautiful painted chairs—Italian, French, and English—in various stages of flaking. A handsome Venetian sofa, an early purchase from Hollyhock, is now covered in cream silk velvet with lavender undertones that looks rather moth-eaten—something both Courtnay and I find charming. Many of the other colors were taken from a French document cotton whose chinoiserie figures and overscale flowers are printed in odd shades of pale orange, pink, and green, and which covers a few chairs. The walls are a soft green, and we kept the original, faintly striped oyster-colored silk curtains on the orangerie-style windows.

This is really one of the prettiest rooms I have ever been in. A pair of Italian tables, found long ago in San Francisco, is topped with slate so that pots of flowering shrubs from the greenhouse can sit on them. Everything is reflected in two large mirrors that I had made from rectangles of glass rolled the same way it was done in the eighteenth century, so that reflections are softly distorted. During the day, the mirrors magnify the light from the arched windows—beautifully dappled through the old oak trees outside—and at night, the candlelight.

A view of the living room from a terrace under the old oaks. The room was once a porch, and acres of beautiful Virginia countryside are visible through its arched windows. RIGHT: The dappled afternoon light falls upon a collection of early nineteenth-century dragée boxes and confiture jars found at French flea markets that hold candles. The distortions of the mouth-blown glass and hand-rolled mirrors softly reflect sunlight or candlelight.

The mellow textures of this room contribute to its beauty—the braided straw of the rug over the waxed-brick floor, the painted paper of the bandbox made into a table, the flaking paint and gently tarnished gilt of the furniture, and the sparkling crystal chandelier. Even the smooth, printed cottons and velvet look beautifully timeworn. A carved acanthus leaf on a Federal marble mantel inspired the design of the embroidery on the wool-satin tablecloth. Light shines through the unlined silk curtains.

One of a pair of contemporary mirrors pieced together from rectangles of rolled glass reflects a lead urn filled with flowers from the gardens. The urn sits on an eighteenth-century Italian painted table that has been scraped back to its original pale-blue color. A canapé with straight legs and a chair with curved ones are two of many old painted pieces in the room. RIGHT: On a tall stand is a nineteenth-century leech jar that now holds a candle. A neoclassical carved-stone head quietly looks down from the wall.

The library sits at one end of the house, and has windows on three sides that look onto the gardens and the pasture. It is the most Williamsburg-looking of the rooms at Whilton Farm, with its beautiful paneling of classical proportions. The paneling, the finely carved pilasters, the cornice molding, and the handsome fireplace surround were all painted in one of three different shades of white to emphasize their detailing. This is a Georgian device that I first read about in that most interesting and useful book *English Decoration in the Eighteenth Century* by John Cornforth and John Fowler. I have learned a great deal from that publication, as well as from Ann and Alan Gore's *The History of English Interiors*. Ann's illustrated talks always fascinate me, as they illuminate the ways people lived their everyday lives and how that is expressed through their furniture and decorations.

The library is a cozy and relaxing room, full of the books and sporting paintings that are hallmarks of the house. There is a squashy sofa covered in a classic dark-brown toile de Jouy, La Dame du Lac, and the room's numerous chairs, most being one of a kind, are covered in leather or wool. The pair of hanging lights are old tole ones, painted with symbols, perhaps from some long-gone secret society.

On the other side of the entry hall is the family sitting room. The television resides in here so the sofa is incredibly deep and wonderful for lying down on and watching football or a movie. There are Napoleon III madame and monsieur chairs, one slightly larger than the other, and both are buttoned and very comfortable. The walls are painted a bleached pine *faux bois*, with trompe l'oeil paneling on the wainscot and hidden doors. Swedish painted tables, beautiful Chinese painted panels, and Christopher Spitzmiller lamps all contribute to the serene feeling of the room.

Two tufted ribbed-velvet chaise longues flank the library fireplace with a fine lacquered Chinese low table between them to hold books or a drink. It is wonderful to stretch out and read alone on one of the chaises, or, when the library is the scene of after-dinner drinks or charades, they become perches for several people. Four painted Swedish chairs, upholstered in glazed linen, surround an antique Italian table with eccentric legs used for puzzles or card games. On the shelves is a collection of books about horses, fox hunting, and life in the country.

Courtnay's private study is off the family's sitting room. Here she has baskets of catalogs and correspondence surrounding her antique Italian desk with long legs. Photographs of family and friends crowd the surface, and favorite sporting paintings hang over it and around the room. RIGHT: The next-door sitting room is a family gathering place, with its television and comfortable seating and soft colors. The Hollyhock Racetrack ottoman is slipcovered and so invites you to put up your feet. The diamond-striped rug is chic and practical tufted coir, perfect for indoor/outdoor country life.

Places to Eat

The dining room at Whilton is used for celebratory dinners, but seeing it every day as you traverse the house acts as an elixir, as there are so many specially chosen objects to delight the eye. A beautiful mirror with an unusual topknot that used to be installed in the master bedroom now hangs above a Louis XVI canapé that has always lived against this wall. The antique mirrored Venetian sconces on either side reflect the crystal chandelier, too. The chairs around the table—bought long ago from a dealer on London's King's Road—are Regency, with

their original painted flowers and decorations in blue and rose on dirty white. Against one wall is an architectonic cabinet of waxed pine filled with Napoli ware in different lettuce-leaf shapes that Courtnay has collected over the years. Colorful Regency porcelains usually decorate the table, rather than flowers. The floor was painted in a diamond design by Bob Christian. On either side of the door are glimpses of the serpentine hall that he painted in the style of nineteenth-century *papier peint*. It is subtly aged to look as if it has been there since the early part of the last century.

Flowering kale, chosen from the kitchen garden for its form and strong-green color, makes an unusual arrangement in an Old Paris tureen on the sideboard. RIGHT: A view of the dining room from the serpentine hall, which was painted to resemble a *papier peint* wall covering. The rich surface of the dining table is left bare as a foil for the brightly colored porcelain.

When we redecorated, some changes were made to the kitchen. The island was shortened—so many are too large—which allowed us to add a handsome antique French draper's table with brass supports, perfect for setting out a breakfast buffet for a house party or displaying a group of old marble mortars with pestles. RIGHT: We kept the family's classic French brass-bound fruitwood table, and added Hollyhock's comfortable Robin chairs to pull up around it. Favorite sporting paintings were also hung in this room so the family could enjoy them more often. The wide pine floorboards are treated with oil and look better the more they are used.

The Laundry
and Pantry

At one end of the kitchen is a traditional butler's pantry, as well as a fabulous closet made from a quirky passageway that once led to the serpentine hallway connecting the entry to the dining room. This is the kind of space that can sometimes be reclaimed in old houses, and we were happy when a friend made the suggestion. It is well lit and contains painted shelves on curved supports above closed cupboards or bars—a clever way to hang tablecloths, quilts, and throws. The shelves hold a miscellany of glasses, carafes, platters, plates, vases, and coffee cups. It is a joy to go into that room and be able to see at a glance what you might want for the table. Nearby is the butler's pantry that has always served the kitchen. It holds glasses and plates for everyday use and many different baskets.

The mudroom, at the other end of the kitchen, leads out to the side garden. This is where you enter the house after being in the garden and where the laundry is done. Courtnay kept the great old soapstone sinks that have always been here and added an old-fashioned ceiling-mounted clothes-drying device that is worked by pulleys. Cupboards hold boots and hats, and there is an amusing collection of Victorian taxidermy.

A closet made from an unused passageway is filled with fascinating items for the table, from unusual glasses, platters, and carafes to linens. It is well lit and lined with old-fashioned shelves. Everything is out in the open, immediately visible, and easy to reach.

The nineteenth-century soapstone sinks in the mudroom are still used. Laundry is hung to dry on an old-fashioned rack-and-pulley device. RIGHT: The original butler's pantry, where the plates and glasses the family uses every day are kept. A zinc ram's head sits on an old column, one of the many objects that delight the eye throughout the house.

The Boudoir

The last rooms Courtnay and I reimagined at Whilton Farm were the master bedroom and the adjoining bathroom, dressing room, and narrow hall. More closets were needed, and Courtnay wanted a more spacious dressing area. The inspiration came from seeing the Florida house where the stylish tastemaker K. K. Auchincloss lived. It had been designed by the architect F. Burrell Hoffman, for himself and his wife, and had many marvelous features, including a double-cube living room. The idea that sparked our imaginations was the placement of closets in the four corners of the master bedroom. Hoffman designed his closets with French boiserie, while we engaged Bob Christian to paint these in a very fanciful way.

Building those closets and the pair flanking the dressing table freed up a good deal of space for a more gracious room—a boudoir—that just happens to in-corporate a bathroom. The dressing table is used every day and is practical as well as beautiful, with a mirror that had been at Ditchley, one of Nancy Lancaster's famous houses. On the opposite side is a curving wall, behind which is the bath. Water falls into the bateau-shaped bath from an eighteenth-century Italian iron water urn, its *faux marbre* base fitted with contemporary bronze spigots. I have always loved these kinds of urns and bought them when I could for Hollyhock. This one was the starting point for the bath and everything else grew from that idea.

Bob Christian painted a *papier peint*–style mural behind the tub, similar to an old wallpaper that Frédéric Méchiche, the French designer, had used in his own bath in Paris, the inspiration for this room. All of the floors are herringbone in a gray wash. There are many colors in the room, but most of them, except for the baseboards painted in a Siena marble, are soft ones.

A beautiful dressing table, flanked by terra-cotta allegories of spring and summer, in the anteroom of the master bedroom. FOLLOWING PAGES: Opposite the anteroom is a curved wall behind which stands the bateau bath that is filled from an old Italian urn. Nearby is this narrow console with an exuberant bronze candlestick adorned with flowers and hounds. Just behind is the trompe l'oeil painted cabinet fitted with a sink.

This room features a good part of Courtnay's collection of eighteenth-century women's pastimes pictures. Many are dressed pictures, with bits of metallic and silk fabrics and paper adorning the gouache or engraved figures. Some are reverse-glass paintings, and others are miniature watercolors of Italian landscapes from the Grand Tour. A few French pastel portraits are hung here, as well. The painted English chair was bought at auction in Switzerland. We took great pains with the details of these curtains, though all are quite simple. Below the Italian mirror on the curving wall is a panel that allows access to the plumbing, disguised as a painted roundel. RIGHT: Near the tub, an Edwardian pastry table stands beside a chaise longue that looks out over the countryside.

The Bedrooms

Courtnay has always loved the idea of a bit of drama and theatrics in the decor of her bedroom. The ceilings are very high, as the couple had already incorporated part of the attic in a previous renovation. A wonderful taupe color covers the walls, energized with Bob's imaginative painting of flora and fauna in soft greens, creams, and browns. He painted the corner closets like canopies.

Contrasting elements in the room give it interest. An old Virginia mantel, stripped of its paint, stands out against the rich walls, and a luxurious satin-covered banquette with burnished-metal fringe becomes even more elegant when placed on a raffia-and-cotton rug.

Both Courtnay and I have always loved a *lit à la polonaise*, from the fanciest French to the simplest Swedish. This was a chance to create a variation of the simple steel bed I designed for Hollyhock, but with great height and a curving top. The severity of the metal and the generosity of the dressmaker curtains with the accordion-pleated edges make a stunning combination. The silk is a quiet blue but woven with two colors so it is subtly lively. Everything else about the bed and the room is tailored. The sheets are simple, the blanket cover is quilted, and the gorgeous feather duvet is held together with classic fabric knots. The rest of the furniture is severe neoclassical, both Swedish and Italian.

Down the hall is a guest room, dominated by an eighteenth-century painted linen hanging found in Paris. We were told that these hangings are copies of tapestries that Parisians had in their town houses. They would take these copies to their country houses where it was too hot to use a tapestry. To me, the copies are more charming than the real thing. In addition to this piece, the room contains a couple of pastel portraits. All of the beautiful colors we used were inspired by these pieces of art. Below the linen hanging is another Chinese low table, piled with interesting books and magazines.

More guest rooms for children and grandchildren are farther down the hall. All are furnished simply, with thoughtful bedding and interesting pictures. Each grandchild has a monogrammed pillow put on his or her bed when visiting.

A view of the master bedroom with the old Virginia mantel, stripped of pigment, placed against the deep-taupe walls painted with fanciful flowers and birds. The settee is covered in satin, and the rug is raffia and cotton. The exceptionally high ceiling encouraged a certain theatricality in the decoration. The old chandelier once hung in a French church.

The bed curtains are made of unlined silk and self-trimmed in fabric we had accordion pleated. The silk is substantial so it falls in gorgeous exuberance, in contrast to the severe steel beds and tailored bedding. Although the silk is a soft blue, it is woven with two colors, so it has remarkable vitality.

Here is one of the bedrooms for grandchildren, tucked under the eaves. Courtnay has been collecting single Swedish beds for some time and furnishes their rooms with them. This one has been fitted with a trundle. These rooms are cozy, with walls covered in a Japanese corrugated paper and the floors in wall-to-wall woven-linen carpeting. The soothing, textured background is punctuated with examples from Courtnay's remarkable collection of eighteenth-century pinprick pictures and needlework, and some wonderful painted country chairs.

The Garden and the Out Buildings

At Whilton Farm, the beauty of the countryside and the beauty of the gardens seem to integrate effortlessly. Trees are planted just beyond the gardens, in the fields where hunting horses once pastured, making the beginnings of an arboretum. They create a fine transition from the cultivated to the wild.

Over the years, the gardens have grown to fifteen acres, and as they have changed, so have the ideas that inspired them. Very few of the herbaceous perennials that occupied much of the initial gardens remain. The beds are less about flowers and more about the subtle gradations of the colors and shapes of leaves and the mass of shrubs and trees. Courtnay was trained as a painter and she now paints with plants. There is an apricot garden, a yellow garden, a kitchen garden, and a conifer garden.

A Southern vernacular cottage serves as the garden studio. Filled with light, it is built in an H shape, and contains an extensive reference library at one end and an office at the other. Here is where the computers, complete with a GPS system, keep track of each new shrub and tree. There are inspiration boards studded with great pictures, and all kinds of gardening and botanical books.

Next door is the marvelous double-height potting shed, flanked by greenhouses. It has a great-looking and practical brick floor and is lined with cupboards to hold garden paraphernalia. Old garden tools decorate the walls, and the storage is topped with a growing collection of old watering cans. From the potting shed and the garden studio, you can easily access the trial fields in the back, where new plants are kept until Courtnay and her ace team of Polly McConnell and Lois Smith are certain they understand where each will best prosper. Leave by the front door and you enter a series of gardens that lead you all around the property.

A clapboard cottage houses the garden office. The sun pours in through French windows onto the painted stripes of the floor, where a working lunch is set out. The dining table is placed in the narrow part of the H-shaped structure, with a reference library and desks with computers at either end. Various pieces of furniture that Courtnay loves have found their way into this workroom.

A pinup board holds pictures of ongoing garden projects, as well as inspirations. A pile of books for research sits on the wicker table next to a French fauteuil. The computers record the botanical names and location of every plant in the gardens. RIGHT: The double-height potting shed is lined with cupboards to store garden paraphernalia. A collection of old garden implements decorates the space, and an eighteenth-century Italian terrarium sits on the counter.

Dinner or drinks in the gazebo is the perfect place for viewing the enchanting colors of this perennial garden. RIGHT: A long French farm table is set for a summer supper on the grassy walkway to the barn. An allée of maples (*Acer rubrum* 'October Glory') within the black-stained fences provides a shady retreat from the sun. Local produce, fresh and colorful and simple and delicious, is ready as a first course. The table is set with glass and pottery picked up at flea markets and interesting local shops.

The gazebo is often the site of lunch or dinner. The view is through clipped walls of hornbeam to a plinth with a bust whose head lies beside him. The foothills of the Blue Ridge Mountains lie beyond the pastures. RIGHT: A small corner of the yellow garden, composed of bulbs, trees, and flowering shrubs. The table is set for a summer supper for three. An old hand-loomed linen sheet, Napoli ware plates, and beautiful glass, old and new, add to the atmosphere.

SEASIDE ESCAPE

Driving through the quiet entrance to Sunsong—down a gravel path edged with high walls of dark-green tropical foliage, around a large banyan tree banked with selloum philodendron and hung with different kinds of orchids—it becomes clear that this property is an enchanted remnant of Old Florida. The raised cottage that greets you, with its restrained facade and soft-blue doors, was built in the 1940s. It still retains its original, unpretentious paneling and high wood-planked ceilings, as well as its engaging charm.

The architectural scale and details of the original house so captivated Courtnay and Terry Daniels that they chose to make it a place just for the two of them. Rather than building one Brobdingnagian house to accommodate their family and friends, they decided that visitors would stay in the existing guesthouse and a new cottage, to be built in a simple, southern Florida vernacular. The three structures are well sited on the property, with foliage from the garden providing privacy. All of them are frequently filled with family and friends, so there are numerous places at Sunsong to read, play cards and games, swim, and just loll.

Courtnay, my great friend and client, is knowledgeable about furniture and the decorative arts, and she is well traveled—so when I propose something a little offbeat, she is never afraid. Right away, we decided that the house would be designed with Florida colors—not the usual vibrant ones, but those inspired by the sand, sea, and sky of the area. In the front rooms, we found the ceilings already painted blue—like the ceilings of many Southern porches—and we simply softened the color. Most of the walls seemed right with a traditional whitewash, and all of the floors were painted in the café-au-lait shades of seashells, in different marvelous patterns, by decorative painter Bob Christian of Savannah.

Before Sunsong, I had never designed an entire house with painted floors, though I have always adored them. I still have a vivid memory of seeing for the first time pictures of Sybil Connolly's Mews House in Dublin, where her fortunate guests stayed. The Mews House floors were painted as interlocking octagonal shapes in soft colors. Stripped and waxed pine trim further lightened the room, whose cornice was decorated with plaster casts from a scallop shell given to her by Tony Duquette. It was a perfect backdrop for the chintz-covered upholstered pieces and attractive old furniture that filled up the room. My response was total capitulation to Connolly's charming vision.

I had the same reaction upon seeing photographs of Pauline de Rothschild's famous rooms, which she and John Fowler created, at Albany, in London. They were decorated with painted floors of *faux marbre* or geometric patterns, and furnished with a few fine antiques. My husband's and my first house had stenciled bedroom floors of blues and white. These remain favorite rooms of mine, though they are long gone. At Sunsong, we set about capturing a feeling of beautiful relaxation, and the painted floors were integral to this.

The entrance to Sunsong—a name the house has had for some time. RIGHT: The strong, simple painted paneling in the octagonal entry hall sets the welcoming tone. The sun—inspired by period engravings—is painted in sandy shades of cream and brown. Directoire chairs flank the entry, along with old lacquered cabinets on stands. An oval mirror atop a stripped Louis XV console reflects a charming Italian trompe l'oeil painted tole clock—one of several eighteenth- and nineteenth-century Continental theater props throughout the house.

The living room is washed with lovely indirect lighting during the day, which enhances the colors we used—sky, sand, and ocean hues, mixed with the soft coral, lavender, and brown shades of seashells. Near the fireplace, two sofas are slipcovered in hand-blocked chintz from Mrs. Monro that incorporates many of these colors. A pair of Louis XVI slipper chairs is upholstered in a narrow coral-and-white stripe, and the tufted ottomans are made up in cocoa-colored twill. This room says a lot about the owners' taste—the very comfortable slip-covered sofas, the interesting and amusing books at hand from their well-chosen collection, attractive antique chairs to pull up wherever you want for conversation, and delightful objects to look at everywhere. Among my favorites are the quirky, graphic, Continental mirror over the fireplace mantel and the Old Paris porcelain perfume bottles shaped as shells that sit atop it. The Regency table in front of the other sofa sits on a swooping stand, its top painted in watercolor butterflies.

Many unusual objects were collected for Sunsong, and we gave them room to breathe. Sitting on a Swedish chest of drawers are the patron saints of the house, two Italian reliquaries with peeling paint, found in the countryside of France. They often are surrounded by orchids, but at Christmastime are decorated with wreaths of boxwood and kumquats. The furniture comes from several countries, and almost all of it is neoclassical in style, whether French, Italian, or English. The surfaces are varied, some stained and polished or stripped, while others are lacquered to a shine or have timeworn paint.

The leggy eighteenth-century furniture contributes to the airy and serene feel of this room, as does the painted-diamond floor. The far doors are surrounded by original columns and woodwork whose details inspired us to repeat them elsewhere in the house. Beyond them are broad steps that lead to a coquina-shell dining patio.

The seventeenth-century portrait was bought for the subject's attitude of dash and swagger, and for the beautiful big cockades on his shoes. Both the demilune cabinet and the candelabra are Italian and have mates on the other side of the windows. RIGHT: Across from the fireplace is another comfortable sofa, covered in sky-blue cotton, and an Italian painting flanked by Continental gilt-and-crystal-beaded sconces, and one of a pair of drawings. The Gustavian painted armchairs are covered in glazed linen.

Dining Around the House

Courtnay believes that meals with friends and family should be a celebration of life. The marvelously fresh and simple dishes she prepares, often influenced by her extensive travels through Asia, are served in several different spots at Sunsong. In the dining room, she holds dinners for large numbers of friends, places set with oversized pale-cocoa plates and amethyst glasses for Thai food and California wine. She likes to set a special lunch for two on the smaller French table at the end of the room and prepare simple pasta with fresh vegetables and Parmesan, presented on unusual armorial dishes. Drinks will likely be served on one of the terraces, with dinner *al fresco* on the patio a few steps down from the living room.

In the morning, there is a "help yourself" breakfast of juice, bread and jam, and yogurt and fruit set out on the old patisserie table that serves as an island in the kitchen. Everyone drops in and out for morning papers and conversation before setting off for golf, tennis, or simply to lie on a chaise longue. Creamware is used for breakfast, along with great-looking glasses and mugs from French country markets and inexpensive shops. A casual breakfast for the family will be set out as simply and carefully as one for houseguests. When you have collected things that you love, and feel comfortable using them, it is easy to really enjoy life every day, not just at dinner parties.

Courtnay and I took great care in designing the back-of-house working spaces: the kitchen, the pantry, and storage areas that are so important to making everyday living easy and enjoyable. We worked on them during family vacations, when we would take our children to a lovely house in Beaulieu-sur-Mer. One of the children's enduring memories is of the two of us in the shallow end of the pool, with giant cartwheel hats shielding us from the sun, bent over architectural plans as we designed the kitchen.

A collection of shells in all shades of brown inspired the colors of the floors. Here in the dining room, Bob Christian painted large *faux marbre* octagonals. The cabinet is grained to look like rosewood, a favorite English Regency device, and decorated in gilding with neoclassical figures—the perfect foil for a collection of sepia-decorated creamware. The coral used in the living room is repeated on the stripes of the French painted chairs.

We closed up a bar and extended the dining room, copying the simple columns in the living room to delineate the spaces. A Continental theater prop—a column—leans against a wall. Glass-topped skirted sideboards with appliquéd Greek keys at the hem stand opposite each another. The amethyst from the living room was continued with an antique bell light. RIGHT: The Italian urn-shaped candelabra, one of a pair, was bought by Courtnay in a London shop whose owner told her he had found them in Florida—good things travel around. The marvelous Italian chinoiserie wallpaper panels, a later find, were hung behind them.

A table is set for lunch using a collection of old beakers, William Yeoward bistro flutes, odd pieces of silver and creamware, and speckled shells for salts. RIGHT: In the smaller part of the dining room, a beautiful eighteenth-century wrought-iron wreath hangs on the wall. It still retains traces of silver leaf and ghostly white paint and moves like a caliper. Below it is a serene papier-mâché sphinx, once used in a French theater. The walls are the same shade as the main part of the room, but here in alternating horizontal stripes of matte and shiny paint.

In the pantry, creamware and drabware are stored in cabinets with pink-coral interiors. The floor is painted a Swedish blue *faux bois* with a scattering of white diamonds. On the bar sit the makings of any drink you could ever want. The antique creamware shells are from France. The painting of a fishmonger with a leek pinned to her bonnet is Welsh. In the breakfast room, the midnight-blue Italian painted metal chandelier, which once held candles, is hung with round crystals. The wall, table, and painted Directoire cabinet display Creil transferware. The vendange table is used for breakfast, the occasional lunch, and for planning menus. Regency painted chairs surround it. RIGHT: We repurposed old windows in the kitchen, placing them at counter level to give views into the Thai-inspired garden, whose design was influenced by the family's travels. The kitchen is inviting and easy to use as it is laid out in the traditional manner. A Napoleon III patisserie table serves as the island.

Retreats

Thinking about how you actually live in your current house and how you might want to live in a new situation will give you valuable clues for planning the rooms. When the Danielses bought Sunsong, they decided to make the main cottage a place just for the two of them. To this end, we set about rearranging some of the private rooms. We transformed the existing guest room and some closets into a wonderful library and sitting room for the master bedroom. The library incorporates bookshelves (where a linen closet and bar used to be) and a handsome old English cabinet with faded chinoiserie decoration that holds the television. There is comfortably upholstered furniture for reading and for watching television and swing-arm lamps and other useful lighting, as this room is often used at night. Little tables for drinks and places for periodicals are strategically placed and, because this is Florida, there are numerous spots for orchid plants from the garden.

The room works perfectly for the couple's needs. Courtnay has a work area—a beautiful Italian desk—with necessary paperwork organized in baskets on the floor, and a laptop and note cards at the ready. Printers, faxes, and other office paraphernalia are housed in a closet. The fine tole column lamp, French mirror, favorite small reverse-glass paintings and drawings, cups for pens, and an attractive basket for research materials all enhance the business of daily life that occurs here. The floor is *faux bois* and the column is vintage painted wood.

The library is next to the bedroom. A linen closet and a bar were combined with the old guest room to create a space for the shelves that hold part of the couple's extensive collection of memoirs and books on gardens, architecture, travel, history, and food. The upholstery is soft cotton or jute. An English cellarette and a Burmese lacquered stand serve as unusual tables.

In the bedroom, two English campaign tables (which could be dismantled quickly to pack for war maneuvers) are used on either side of the bed. Decoupage lamps from the 1950s sit on top. A graceful *lit de repos* sits at the foot of the bed on the octagonal patterned floor. A pair of overscale Sicilian cameos on the wall add an element of surprise. FOLLOWING PAGES: The cut-and-painted-paper collage is an exceptional example of the kind of projects made by women in the English Regency era; it is mounted on a finely painted Regency stand. Above it is a padded and embroidered felt picture from eighteenth-century England. A glimpse of the sitting room is seen through the doorway.

Fabric patterns inspired by old textile docu-
ments are my favorites and the bedroom
features several. The comfortable chairs are
covered in a pattern taken from a French fabric.
All of the details—old needlework cushions, the
striped tole lampshade, sweet painted shelves of
shells—contribute to creating the ambience. A
chinoiserie-decorated small bookcase with a
reverse-glass painted box. A close-up of an early
nineteenth-century painted tole lamp base
and tray. RIGHT: A graphic chest-on-chest,
Italian chairs, and English drawings; a slice of
the library can be seen through the door.

The Guesthouse and the Folly

Across from the main cottage, on the other side of the swimming pool, is a two-story guesthouse that was already on the property. The architecture, with its Chinese Chippendale railings, has a West Indies feel that captures the cool breezes, making it very inviting. We decorated the guesthouse first so that Courtnay and Terry could live there while the other buildings were being worked on.

The main room is furnished with an upholstered sofa, a deep, cushy chair, and several painted French bergères that are easily moved about. A simple antique fruitwood game table is set up for cards and dominoes (which are stored in a gorgeous bone box). The room is colored in calming aquamarines and creams. Pale watercolors and prints and shaped frames with antique "dead" mirrors are placed on the walls. A straw rug on the marble floor brings the antique-filled space down a bit.

There is a small guest room on this floor and a little kitchen stocked with everything you could wish for snack time. The glorious stairwell winds its way up to the main bedroom. On the ground floor are niches with old columns that can be topped with flowers, or greens and citrus during the holidays. A drinks table for nightcaps is set up on a carved and painted base.

The main bedroom at the top of the stairs takes up the entire floor, along with its anterooms. It is large and full of light, with three French windows that open onto the porch. It is extremely comfortable. We furnished the room with pairs of things—painted *bibliothèques* found in New Orleans, great reading chairs covered in a Robert Kime linen, and double-tester beds designed in my studio. An ample chinoiserie-decorated desk sits in the middle of the room—should there be business to attend to—and a glazed-linen-covered ottoman is usually arrayed with the latest magazines. Courtnay's collection of old books, beautiful drawings, screens, and other delightful objects she has found on her travels add interest and beauty to this room.

Beyond the front door of the guesthouse is the curved staircase leading to the bedroom, festooned with its holiday decorations of white flowers, garden greens, and citrus. A decoupage scrapbook picture hangs over a Directoire chair with flaking paint. A drinks table is partially hidden by the railing.

In the main room, comfortable antique French
bergères, upholstered in cottons and linen mixtures, are
teamed with modern upholstery. The antique shaped
frames with "dead" mirrors were bought at auction. The
marble floor runs throughout the first story—we
covered it with a sisal rug in this room. Painted French
consoles, old lead baskets filled with shells and coral,
and the shaped mirrors are paired on either side of the
room. Through the doors is the dramatic staircase.

The planked ceiling and paneling details of the original cottage are repeated in the bedroom. Hand-screened linen covers the comfortable reading chairs that look over the second-story porch to the garden. We designed two tester beds that sit side by side, dressed in a narrow gray-and-white striped fabric. The Chinese screen, drawings, and decorative objects were collected over many years.

The Folly, where the children and grandchildren stay, has easy-to-clean painted floors. Horizontal planked wood walls recall those of simple houses indigenous to the Florida Keys. The lamps were made from antique Italian church candlesticks and the coffee tables were originally designed for plant displays. Each bedroom in the Folly has its own look, by virtue of being furnished with one-of-a-kind finds—interesting lamps, antique mirrors, and Italian *comodini*. RIGHT: We found the old winter garden chairs in Bonnieux, France. The buffet is Swedish, the portrait is Danish, and the table is French.

Living Outdoors

To walk through the garden at Sunsong is to experience a real sense of place. You could only be in the Florida of a sophisticated and well-traveled gardener. The Danielses chose the talented and equally sophisticated Jorge Sanchez of Palm Beach as their landscape architect—he and Courtnay have concocted a magical garden with a variety of places to enjoy.

On one side of the property is an allée of tall palms that leads from a fountain, along a grass walkway, to the Folly, built as a place for the children and grandchildren to stay. Outside of the Folly is a patio hidden by a baffle hedge from the palm allée. Furnished with lounge chairs and tables, the patio has plenty of space for little ones to play.

On the opposite side is a similar space, with the lovely coquina-shell patio off the living room at one end and a roundel of trees surrounding paving made with concentric circles of smooth stones and matte marble at the other. It is furnished with a table and benches. Midway between the two areas is a beautiful old stone trough with an Italian masque that spits water, creating delightful sounds, which can be seen from the pool patio. Clipped magnolias stand out amid beds of *Begonia odorata* and stunning silvery blue cycads in stone pots. Pale coral brugmansia and jasmines spilling over walls are among the many flowers that scent the garden. There is enough all-important negative space to allow the viewer to appreciate the beautiful plantings.

The long allée of palms has a serpentine low hedge of box. A round fountain is at one end and a stone obelisk at the other. FOLLOWING PAGES: The coquina-shell patio is down the steps from the living room, where dinners are often served. Variegated bromeliads in Provençal melon pots decorate the table, set between two William Yeoward amethyst hurricane shades. The clipped shapes of the garden are visible in the background and look wonderful against the sky. The corals of the brugmansia and the amethyst of the glass echo the colors in the main rooms of Sunsong.

One terminus of the garden is this roundel of trees, centered with a table and seating. The ground is decorated with paving made of circles of stones and matte white marble. Silvery blue cycads in stone pots flank an entry. We found the iron basket at the famous French market in L'Isle-sur-la-Sorgue and it is now filled with shells. RIGHT: The old Italian masque is mounted on a plaque of coquina shell, spilling its water into a fine stone casket. The blue flowers of Petrea, various grasses, and clipped evergreens soften the stone and the gravel path.

PIED-À-TERRE

Fred and I have always enjoyed walking in New York, taking in the varied architectural styles and ambience of the different neighborhoods. On the Upper East Side, where Fred grew up, the classical architecture of so many houses, churches, and apartment buildings is a delight to look at while strolling or even hurrying madly by. I have always liked Lexington Avenue, which retains the smaller one-of-a-kind shops and restaurants that make it feel like a real neighborhood. I often told Fred that our weekend house in the country should be an apartment in Manhattan—to no avail—until it seemed we were about to become grandparents of a brand-new New Yorker. Then he went shopping on the Upper East Side and hit the jackpot with the very first apartment he saw.

We like so many things about this apartment. Sunlight pours through the southeast windows of the corner living room and bounces off the lacquered ceiling. And the apartment feels larger than it is because of the enfilade from living room to library to the bedroom, which was originally the dining room, when this space constituted the public rooms of a duplex apartment. The long view ends at a large, old mirror, which makes the space seem to go on forever. And then there are the two wood-burning fireplaces. My husband has been known to say that he would spend his last five dollars on firewood. When we use them—often in the wintertime—we feel truly at home.

When I saw that the living room walls were broken up by double doors and many windows of different sizes, I realized that arranging art would be a challenge. I had the idea to let the walls become the art, and I knew that Bob Christian, from Savannah, was the one to paint them. The inspiration was a sepia-colored eighteenth-century Italian landscape paper but I didn't want our walls to be quite that serious. Rather I was looking for the imagery to be slightly eccentric, wacky even, which suits Bob's painting style. The floors were yellow oak so I asked him to paint those, too. At first I was taken aback by the freewheeling entry floors that he came up with, thinking they might be too strong for the Italian painted cabinet I planned to put in that space, but I have come to love the juxtaposition of the two.

Our house in Los Angeles is full of color and serendipitous furniture arrangements. I wanted this New York getaway to be serene and more restrained in color, and to have a dash of the city's glamour without the glitz. At the same time, this apartment is not simply a place to crash when we are in New York. I wanted it to be supremely comfortable, and accommodating to life with our family and friends.

The living room walls create a soft café-au-lait background that is calming. The floor is painted in shades of gray with a gray, sisal rug bound in leather. The curtains are taupe. The sofa is upholstered in velvet that is a mixture of brown, purple, and gray, and the Italian gilt and the Louis XV chairs are covered in mellow greens. Other colors in the room include pale camel, pink-ochre, and silver. I used several fabrics on the "wrong" side, including an elaborate woven silk, whose bright colors became more nuanced on the caned chairs around the table.

My fantasy spot in the living room is a Louis XVI chaise longue that is "longue, longue longue," where I plan to reread all the special books I brought from our house in California. Its length makes it possible for a couple of people to perch on it for cocktails, and it is placed next to the very comfortable sofa. I found a 1950s Bagues coffee table with a deep red lacquered top, and sadly, a huge water stain that had turned part of the top bright pink. I soaked it with Old English Scratch Cover, my mother's "fix-all" for furniture, and now the two colors blend beautifully, without that "just restored" look.

A view of the restrained facade of our apartment building. RIGHT: The Bagues sconces from my husband's childhood home in New York are affixed to walls covered in squares of painted Chinese paper; the ceiling and cove are covered in tarnished tea paper. A Dutch kettle stand sits in front of the Gustavian settee upholstered in gauffraged silk.

Behind the sofa is an eighteenth-century table with delicate hoof feet that I had bleached to add a different surface color to the room. It is good for spreading out projects on or for serving dinner—an extension allows seating for ten people, but that is beyond my ken at this point, though perhaps not forever. Fred is determined that we will cook together, the way we used to, and have one of the few kitchens that is actually used in New York. For now, we assemble meals, making some dishes and buying others, though he has already made his delicious roast chicken a few times.

A more frequently used spot for dinner—and breakfast and lunch—is the round table in the corner of the room. It is perfectly positioned for my husband to eat breakfast, read the newspaper, watch morning television, and have a computer running, all at the same time. The tabletop sits on a fabulous English Regency base of fierce and funny serpents, black and gilt. It is where we eat alone and with friends, and play dominoes and intense games of cards.

Although I like to bring foliage and flowers from the garden into the house, New York City apartments obviously require a different strategy. I found that in the course of my daily walks up and down Lexington Avenue to visit our little granddaughter, I couldn't resist perusing the corner deli flower stands. Amid the dyed blue flowers and ubiquitous tight roses, there is always something interesting to buy a bit of—purple hyacinths, pale amaryllis, green berries—to put into the small vessels I cherry-picked from our cupboards in Los Angeles. One large vessel I brought was a Regency patinated metal water urn, whose spout I had removed and sealed. This is a trick I learned from seeing the ones that my friend Ann Gore, the social historian, inherited from John Fowler. The tube where the hot coals went to warm the water makes an excellent frog to hold larger branches. I buy tall bunches of magnolia leaves in the winter, and pittosporum branches and maybe hydrangeas in the summer. If I am only in New York for a few days, the graceful top goes on the urn and it becomes a lovely object.

The Italian painted cabinet was an impulsive purchase immediately after we bought the apartment. It set the tone for what was to come. The silver clamshells set on it hold lights that illuminate the eighteenth-century portrait of a lady as Flora. Farther down the hall are four unusual *dessins habillés* of Turks. The exuberant painted floor creates a lively contrast to the rest of the entrance hall.

The living room is serene, with its painted sepia walls, inspired by old *papier peint* panels, but with more eccentric imagery. The chairs are period, the ones with cushions capacious and comfortable. The bronze legs of the lacquered coffee table; the painted, gilded, stained, and waxed wood surfaces; and the various fabric textures bring a subtle interest to the room. The floor is covered with matte-gray sisal and the ceiling is lacquered off-white, to reflect the light.
FOLLOWING PAGES: The wing chairs were recent presents from my mother, icons of my childhood house in the 1950s. They sit on either side of an Italian desk that is also flanked by two pale ochre French garden statues, Diana the Huntress and an allegory of hope. The Georgian mirror is one of a pair.

I am mad about the Regency table base and had a marbled wooden top made for it; I placed sturdy nineteenth-century Louis XV–style chairs around it. The woven fabric for the cushions was used on the reverse to quiet the pattern and colors. The curtains are of Lee Jofa Glazed Silk, embroidered in chenille by Michael Savoia, from a pattern in the Jansen archive. RIGHT: We love feeding our friends. Here the table is set for three, with Kangxi plates and contemporary Venetian glasses.

The living room in its summer guise.
Slipcovers in my City Stripe in charcoal
and oyster, natural-colored candles instead
of my wintertime black ones, and garden
flowers such as hydrangeas and clematis.
The summer cushions are in gray lavender,
pale apricot, and offbeat pastels.

Our bar is arranged on a tole tray atop an eighteenth-century Dutch mahogany chest of drawers with a trompe l'oeil cabinet in the front and a Classical Revival "foot" of talons holding rods. The copper shows through on the finely scribed monogram of this Sheffield silver cup, which holds a cool-looking summer arrangement of variegated pittosporum. RIGHT: The arm of this eighteenth-century Italian chair is a thing of beauty to me, its gilding worn just enough. Clematis fills an old glass next to the Egyptian Revival candlestick. On the bleached oak table, a silver tray with Chinese export cups painted with seaweed bladders. A detail of the chenille embroidery on the living room curtains.

The Enfilade

The library is an entirely cosseting room. Most of the upholstered pieces, as well as the walls, are covered in one of my designs, a linen-and-wool jacquard weave in silvery beige. A woven linen rug bound in a narrow leather band cushions the floor. An extra-deep Edwardian-style club chair, a Hollyhock design, and Jonas Upholstery's Syrie Maugham sofa provide utter comfort for reading, watching television, or napping. Two étagères on either side of the door to the bedroom were made to hold the television and the art and architecture books I brought from our house in California. It is a cozy place to have dinner on a tray in front of the fire, or to read stories to our granddaughter.

The bedroom is almost always open to the other rooms, and so I did not want it to look too "bedroomy." What you see through the doors is a very large Louis XVI mirror (a happy mistake—I bought it at auction after only seeing it in the catalog, and thought it was much smaller) flanked by two Provençal columns brought from our Back House in Los Angeles. The reflection in its original plate gives a dreamy, seemingly endless perspective. Two period slipper chairs finally landed here, ideal for putting on socks and boots.

Our bedroom has plenty of closets, as we were able to make a dressing room, with a capacious shower and a separate loo, out of a miniscule maid's bedroom and bath. A small room in the middle contains the sink and cabinet. Chuck Hettinger, a New York decorative painter, expertly stenciled this little room to look as though it were upholstered and buttoned. The floor is radiant heated, a luxury I would choose over gilded anything any day.

When we converted the maid's room, a doorway was removed, making the kitchen arrangement more workable and yielding more space. One side is used for floor-to-ceiling built-in storage, with doors that hide a washer and dryer, a broom closet, a large pantry with electrical outlets, and a shallow space that we use for a foldout ironing board. The other side of the room is for cooking and washing up. The kitchen is simply designed and works like a dream.

A Louis XVI mirror in the bedroom anchors the end of the enfilade, its reflection making the rooms seem even more spacious. Eighteenth-century Provençal columns and painted slipper chairs flank it. An Emilio Terry umbrella stand is packed with moss and French tulips for a party.

The library walls and furniture are covered in pale French Paisley to evoke a quiet feeling. The exception is the French chair from Tony Duquette's estate that is covered in Elsie, an animal-print velvet, and the Rose Cummings double-cushion ottoman. I love everything about the Chinese table in front of the sofa—its size, shape, age, and the patina of the beautiful wood.

An eighteenth-century Italian wood carving of fronds is mounted above the French neoclassical fire surround. Ancient Khmer shell earrings and a Chinese export jug with flowers sit on the ledge. A bronze Buddha, a French confectionary urn, and a terra-cotta pot full of hellebores rest on a mahogany table. Two watercolors, a Russian interior by James Steinmeyer and an antique one of a man and his dog, hang above an Italian inlaid worktable that holds the telephone. RIGHT: The Syrie Maugham sofa makes a prime napping spot. The drawing by Janine Janet was bought at auction in Paris and saved for New York. I thought this image of a sheep hung with crystals was perfect for the city.

Wall-to-wall carpeting in the bedroom ensures quiet. Partial curtains on the iron beds further the feeling of warm comfort. They are made of the same City Stripe in honey as the window curtains. I brought some of my flower paintings, mostly old, to hang on the walls. A favorite contemporary painting by Charles Masson hangs on the right. Above the door is a terra-cotta head, with the view to the living room beyond.

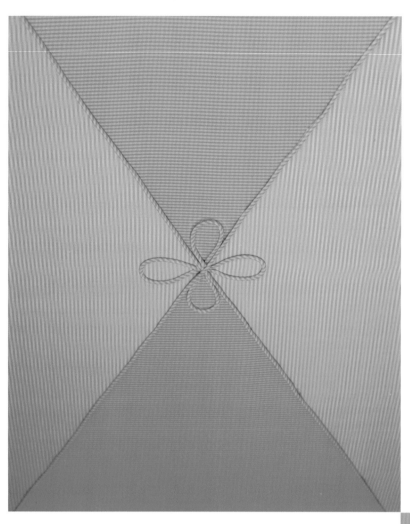

The bed's tester has mitered stripes and a narrow rope trim. The tole container is French nineteenth century, with five tiers and exuberant *faux bois* decoration. I love it filled with purple clematis. The front of the letter holder is a three-dimensional scene made from an old engraving. RIGHT: French and English floral watercolors hang above an Italian chest of drawers that retains its original paint. Through the door on the right is the dressing room and bathroom.

The small room at the center of the dressing room, shower, and loo contains the sink. The mirror opens to the medicine cabinet, and the antiqued silver-leaf frame remains stationary. The walls seemed too icy, so they were stenciled to look as though they are buttoned. RIGHT: The kitchen is a traditional design with marble counters and brick behind the stove. On the left are floor-to-ceiling cabinets. The floors were painted in a lighthearted imitation of marble planks. Antique tin-glazed plates, in my favorite blue and white, decorate the wall.

Design Inspirations and Resources

INSPIRATIONS

HOUSE MUSEUMS
AND GARDENS
EUROPE:

Sir John Soane's Museum
London, England
www.soane.org

Uppark
West Sussex, England
www.nationaltrust.org.uk

Vaux-le-Vicomte
Maincy, France
www.vaux-le-vicomte.com

Villa del Balbianello
Lake Como, Italy
www.fondoambiente.it/en

Villa Kérylos
Beaulieu-sur-Mer, France
www.villa-kerylos.com

HOUSE MUSEUMS
AND GARDENS
UNITED STATES:

The John P. Humes Japanese
Stroll Garden
Mill Neck, New York
www.gardenconservancy.org

Longue Vue House and Gardens
New Orleans, Louisiana
www.longuevue.com

Monticello
Charlottesville, Virginia
www.monticello.org

The Pearl Fryar
Topiary Garden
Bishopville, South Carolina
www.fryarstopiaries.com

Vizcaya Museum & Gardens
Miami, Florida
www.vizcayamuseum.org

Wave Hill Garden
Bronx, New York
www.wavehill.org

ORGANIZATIONS OFFERING
TOURS OF PRIVATE
HOUSES AND GARDENS

French Heritage Society
www.frenchheritagesociety.org

The Garden Conservancy
www.gardenconservancy.org

Historic Charleston Foundation
www.historiccharleston.org

Institute of Classical Architecture
& Classical America
www.classicist.org

The Royal Oak Foundation
www.royal-oak.org

IN MY LIBRARY

Fowler, John and John Cornforth. *English Decoration in the Eighteenth Century.* London: Barrie and Jenkins, 1974.

Gere, Charlotte. *Nineteenth-Century Decoration: The Art of the Interior.* New York: Harry N. Abrams Inc., 1989.

Gore, Ann and Alan. *The History of English Interiors.* London: Phaidon Press, Ltd., 1991.

Kernan, Thomas. *Collection Maison & Jardin: Nouvelles Réussites de la Décoration Française, 1960-1966.* Paris: Robert Laffont, 1966.

Levallois, Pierre, et al. *Connaisance des Arts: Decoration.* 8 vols. English ed. New York: Hachette, 1963–8.

Leveque, Jacques, ed. *Jansen Decoration.* Paris: Société de publications économique, 1971.

Plumb, Barbara. *Horst: Interiors.* New York: Little Brown and Company, 1993.

Praz, Mario. *An Illustrated History of Furnishing: From the Renaissance to the Twentieth Century.* New York: George Braziller Press, 1964.

Rense, Paige, ed. *Architectural Digest: Celebrity Homes.* Los Angeles: The Knapp Press, 1977.

——. *Architectural Digest: International Interiors.* Los Angeles: The Knapp Press, 1975.

——. *The World of Architectural Digest.* Los Angeles: The Knapp Press, 1975–. Series includes *New York Interiors, California Interiors, Traditional Interiors,* and *Historic Interiors.*

Skurka, Norma. *The New York Times Book of Interior Design and Decoration.* New York: HarperCollins Publishers, 1978.

Vreeland, Diana, and Valentine Lawford. With photographs by Horst. *Vogue's Book of Houses, Gardens, People.* New York: Viking Press, 1968.

RESOURCES

These shops and companies are a few of my favorite resources that are featured in this book.

ARCHITECTS

Design Unit
www.designunitstudio.com

The Jarvis Group Architects, AIA, PLLC
www.jarvis-group.com

Tichenor & Thorp
www.tichenorandthorp.com

CURTAIN WORKROOMS

O'Shea Custom
Van Nuys, California
mboshea@att.net

Valley Drapery and Upholstery
North Hills, California
www.valleydrapery.com

CUSTOM TEXTILES

Sam Kasten
Pittsfield, Massachusetts
www.samkasten.com

DECORATIVE PAINTING

Bob Christian Decorative Art
Savannah, Georgia
www.bobchristiandecorativeart.
com

Chuck Hettinger Painting
New York, New York
212-614-9848

Peter Bolton, Inc.
Los Angeles, California
peterbolton@sbcglobal.net

FABRICS AND TRIMMINGS

Claremont Furnishing
Fabrics Company
www.claremontfurnishing.com

Décor de Paris
www.decordeparis.com

Robert Kime
www.robertkime.com

Suzanne Rheinstein·Hollyhock
for Lee Jofa
www.leejofa.com

FINE EMBROIDERY

Holland and Sherry
(through Mimi London)
Los Angeles, California
www.mimilondon.com

Michael Savoia
Villa Savoia, Inc.
Los Angeles, California
www.villasavoia.net

FURNITURE

Betty Jane Bart Antiques
New York, New York
www.bettyjanebartantiques.com

Evans and Gerst Antiques
West Hollywood, California
www.evansandgerst.com

Gep Durenberger @ J. M.
DuCharme
Henderson, Minnesota
jmducharme@frontier.net

Gerrie Bremermann
New Orleans, Louisiana
www.bremermanndesigns.com

Hollyhock
Los Angeles, California
www.hollyhockinc.com

John Rosselli
New York, New York
www.johnrosselliantiques.com

The Next Notch
Newport Beach, California
949-646-8840

Soniat House Antique Galleries
New Orleans, Louisiana
www.soniatantiques.com

Tom Stansbury Antiques
Newport Beach, California
949-642-1272

Treillage Ltd.
New York, New York
www.treillageonline.com

Uptowner Antiques
New Orleans, Louisiana
www.uptowner.1stdibs.com

LIGHTING

Christopher Spitzmiller
New York, New York
www.christopherspitzmiller.com

UPHOLSTERY

Aixa Fielder Upholstery
Los Angeles, California
aixa2@sbcglobal.net

Jonas Upholstery
New York, New York
www.jonasworkroom.com

Acknowledgments

To Priscilla Wright, who kept this book on track with her organizational skills and
kind encouragement. She still made the time to run Hollyhock.

To Meredy Vranich and to Sarah Miner of the SRA Design Studio, who
contributed in myriad ways and gave me time to write.

To all who have worked at Hollyhock and SRA over the years, especially Joe Nye and Catherine Sidon.

To Michael Boodro, who gave such wonderful advice.

To Doug Turshen, who promised to guide me through the bookmaking process, and did.
He produced a book whose design reflects my aesthetic perfectly.

To Pieter Estersohn, whose extraordinary photographs still make me dream.

To Sandy Gilbert, who made all the pieces come together.

To Charles Miers, for whose vision of my book I am most thankful.

To Margaret Russell whose friendship and steady support through the years
has meant the world to me.

Photography Credits

All photography by Pieter Estersohn with the exception of the following images:

Lynn Brubaker: page 130–131

Tria Giovan: pages 26–27, 160, 164, 180, 186, 188–89, 195, 198, 236, 239

Stefanie Keenan: book jacket author photo

Deanie Nyman: pages 52–53

Tim Street-Porter: pages 22–23, 24 (top, right), 37, 169, 171, 176 (top and bottom, left and top right), 177, 179, 184, 185, 187, 192, 193, 196–197, 200, 201, 202, 206 (bottom, right)

Dominique Vorillon: page 238

William Waldron: pages 127, 134–135, 139, 144

First published in the United States of America in 2010
by Rizzoli International Publications, Inc.
300 Park Avenue South
New York, New York 10010
www.rizzoliusa.com

Project Editor: Sandra Gilbert
Art Direction: Doug Turshen

2014 2015 2016 / 10 9 8 7 6

Printed in China

ISBN-13: 978-0-8478-3409-9

Library of Congress Control Number: 2010927317